PRAISE

"Wow, just wow! [illegible] ce you've all had. I have really enjoyed sharing your [illegible]

"Loved following your journey, ...what a wonderful experience for your children."

"What a fantastic adventure!"

A FAMILY GAP YEAR: EUROPE

A FAMILY GAP YEAR: EUROPE

HOW TO QUIT THE RAT RACE AND SEE THE WORLD WITH YOUR CHILDREN

JODI HAMMOND

For my fellow adventurers: Tim, Toby, Poppy and Rory. May you always have the courage to follow your dreams.

CONTENTS

FOREWORD

In September 2016, my family and I set off on a very big adventure in a very small camper van. Here is the story of how our gap year came about. This book will explain a little more about the what we did along the way, the lessons we learned and how our lives changed as a result of our year away from the rat race. I haven't structured it as a travelogue- mainly because I don't really enjoy reading travelogues. Instead, rather than talk you through month-by-month, county-by-country, I've tried to structure our stories around a few central concepts such as money, schooling and family time. Now that we've got a year's worth of stories to tell, people don't usually want to hear the blow-by-blow account of where we went and what we did. Instead, I find that people want answers to the same sorts of questions: "What was homeschooling like?", "is there something you've learned that will continue to influence your normal lives?", "Was it worth it?", "How much did it cost?", "Did you want to come home again?". It is these questions that form the backbone of my book. I hope you enjoy reading it and that some of you might even be inspired to get out there and see more of the world with your own children.

CHAPTER 1

DECIDING TO QUIT THE RAT-RACE

"You did what?!"

When I first decided to write this book I was watching my three children fly around an overgrown Austrian field on home-made Nimbus 2000s through a huge expanse of knee-deep grass and wild flowers. The background to their fun was a placid lake and, beyond that, a swathe of white-topped Tyrolean mountains. It was half past three in the afternoon, on a Thursday, in April. My husband was sitting, drinking a local beer and whittling more sticks into the wands (requested by the children to expand their magic-making ambitions). Being outside like this, enjoying our surroundings, was how we spent much of our time on our big adventure- after quitting our UK lives, selling our house, packing our three kids into a motorhome and heading off on a big tour of Europe.

I used to be a normal Mum. I used to spend my Thursday afternoons dashing from work to school to swimming lessons, then cooking dinner whilst simultaneously washing ketchup-stained school shirts and making last-minute costumes for tomorrow's World Book Day. After wrestling the kids into bed, I used to wearily welcome my husband home from work, just in time for a quick bite to eat together before taking a shower, sewing some Cubs' badges onto someone's uniform and then falling into bed before it all began again on Friday. I used to be just like everyone else. But then, a little over a year ago, my husband and I decided to take a step away from normal. We decided to change our lives. Even if it was only for one year.

2016 had been a year for quitting things. The UK had voted to quit the European Union. Then David Cameron had quit Downing Street. Nigel Farage left UKIP, Boris Johnson stepped out of the race for PM, Chris Evans quit Top Gear and Roy Hodgson threw in the England manager's towel. Everyone seemed to have had enough. And, as odd a club as that may have seemed, my husband and I decided to join that band of quitters: we left our jobs; sold our house and most of its contents; bought a motorhome; and packed all our remaining worldy-wares (including our three young children) into that small metal box on wheels. In September 2016 we took the ferry across the Channel and set out on a year-long motorhome tour of Europe.

Life is full of people who strike out from the norm isn't it? There will always be free-wheelers and hedonists who follow their dreams and their hearts; hippies who fly in the face of convention and live according to their own free-will. There will always be people who resist settling down into any of the traps of conformity. Tim and I were not those people. On the contrary, we were about as ordinary as it gets. I am a teacher, Tim is a police officer. We had both been working in these professions since finishing university. We'd married young, had three children in fairly swift succession, moved from the suburbs out into the countryside to gain a little more house for our money and we were a good few years into paying off a hefty (but prudent) mortgage. We spent most weekends driving our kids around in sensible, second-hand cars and getting our money's worth from our National Trust membership (a rock and roll weekend might see us indulging in a takeaway to eat in front of the usual TV talent shows). Like I said- boringly normal.

So, what on earth makes two ordinary people do such an extraordinary thing? Why would two stable, professional, parents jack everything in, cast away conformity and go travelling for a year? Well, we were stuck in a rut. A comfortable and happy rut, but a rut nonetheless. Tim and I often found ourselves, in those last tired minutes before sleep, wondering what it was all really about. This 'normal' life we were living. In 2016, our weeks and months were so full of activities and stresses that there was little chance to properly pause and consider what we were really gaining from these relentless spreadsheets we called lives. We realised we wanted more.

HOW IT ALL BEGAN

One day we found ourselves in an unusual situation. Some good friends of ours, who lived a couple of hours' drive away, had just welcomed their first baby into the world and although we were excited to meet their baby, we knew we could not invade their house with our own three noisy offspring in tow. We had powers of recollection enough to realise that a couple in those early days of parenthood would not appreciate us invading their precious, quiet new world with our merry band of under-tens. For once, we set off alone, just Tim and I, travelling speedily up the motorway, during school and nursery hours, racing back for the three o'clock pick-up. This unprecedented few hours alone in the car together gave Tim and I a *very* rare chance to talk, really talk, without the merciless call of hungry kids, after-school clubs and domestic routines.

Sitting in the car with no nursery rhymes, tweeny pop-songs or squabbling to fill the silence, Tim and I found ourselves starting to talk. Proper grown-up talk. Tentatively, I asked my husband "so what *are* our plans for the future?" This was something I'd been dwelling on ever since a recent dinner with lovely friends who were well into a very defined and well-considered long-term plan for their lives. We'd gone out for the evening to celebrate Mrs-Long-Term-Plan's recent promotion to partner of the law firm she works in and as the glasses refilled, our friends had asked us about our own plans for the future. At the time we'd sunk our heads into our wine-glasses, at a bit of a loss for what to say. I think my response was something inarticulate along the lines of "Pfft! You know us, muddling along!" and we laughed it off as silly question. But I'd been thinking about it ever since. Wondering what the truthful answer was. As Tim and I now tried to define our own plan together, on the journey home, we realised we didn't really have one. Tim remembered that we'd had one once:

"Well, back in our twenties we had a plan; we wanted get married, start a family and move out to the countryside."

"But we've done all those things," we realised. To most people minds, I guess we we had been pretty successful. By society's standards we were winning at life. Despite that though, Tim and I found ourselves at a bit of a loss as to where we were headed next. We realised that for a few years we'd simply been getting our heads down and getting on with it. Whatever 'it' was – all we really knew was that it was exhausting.

As a teacher and a civil servant, in austere times, both Tim and I were giving a lot of time and energy to jobs we believed in but which were forever dragging us down into bureaucracy and disillusionment. Our careers, we knew, were not going to lead us to great riches; neither of us were ever going to become partner or CEO. What, we asked ourselves, were we doing all this for? To pay for the childcare and the punishing treadmill of activities that we cajoled our children into 'for their own good'? It suddenly all seemed a little misguided.

At a loss for big career goals, we started to talk about life goals instead. In the previous year, two people close to us had died young. Very young. All of a sudden, our own mortality had become less of a theoretical concept and more of a threatening shadow. We asked ourselves what we wanted from life for our kids and ourselves. The answer was that there were just a few things really: we wanted them to continue enjoying learning for as long as possible; we wanted them to be healthy and happy and we wished that we could afford to travel more. A few weeks' before this conversation, I had been lucky enough to visit Rome on a girls' weekend (laid on by the aforementioned incredibly generous and lovely Mr and Mrs Successful). The trip had reminded me how wonderfully enriching travel can be. I had stood in the Sistine Chapel and remembered what a really big place the world is and how much of its history I just don't know anything about. Tim and I had travelled a bit in our pre-children lives but we were now constrained, as most of us are, by the exorbitantly expensive school holidays. As a result, we hadn't managed to journey very far with our kids. Paying for five flights, plus accommodation, was usually beyond our means. We'd managed a few camping holidays and a couple of house-swaps, which had been great but had usually landed us in more debt and the need to work just a little bit harder (and therefore see the kids a little bit less). We were frustrated by the sudden awareness that one of our long-term goals was to show the children more of the world but simultaneously facing the reality that we couldn't really make that happen.

"I just wish we could pack it all in for a year and take the kids off travelling," Tim sighed carelessly. We stared at the circle of M25 we were stuck in and the dashboard clock that ticked ever closer towards the school pick-up time we were clearly going to be late for. Nice dream.

But there in that traffic jam, an idea had been born.

Ever the optimist, after a few minutes of silence I piped up "You know, we *could* do it."

Tim, the necessary pragmatist, was on hand to counter my recklessness: "Oh yeah, good one! Don't be ridiculous Jodi! People don't do that. How would we afford it? What about schools? What about our jobs? What about the house?" There were a million glaringly obvious reasons why we shouldn't even consider it. Of course there were; you could probably think of twenty reasons right now. It was the world's craziest idea. Despite this, over the course of that car journey my husband and I dared to close our minds, for a moment, to the voices of conformity and found a way that maybe, just maybe, we *could* do it. Of course it was insane. Of course it would be financial suicide to sell our house and take a career break. Of course we couldn't do it-except that we *could.* We really could. It just required a big leap of faith.

We took the leap. A few months later, the 'sold' sign was up, the boxes were packed, we'd bought the motorhome and we were ready to go.

pswclovEU postscript: A little while after we'd made our decision, Brexit happened. The UK voted to leave the European Union. The result shook Tim and I, and many of our friends, into a frenzied and frustrated state of quiet despair. For the two of us, it served only to strengthen our resolve to show our children the beauty of Europe. It also gave us an idea- we could base our trip around the forthcoming loss of our place in the European Union. We would go and see as many EU countries as possible, whilst we were still free to do so. Our journey would be the Hammond family's EU swansong. We'd make it our postscript to a period of time in which people had valued unity and collaboration over prejudice and parochialism. Our pswelovEU tour. It would be both our grand farewell to the European Union and our attempt to rebalance our family's values and experiences. Here is the story of how it panned out. At the end of each chapter, there's a short 'PS Postscript' about what happened once our trip was over.

MAKING IT HAPPEN

Following our Damascene car journey we spent some time looking into the logistics and finances of our hastily-compiled proposal. Tentatively, I called the bank and the estate agents to get some idea of the figures. I started scouring the web for blogs written by people travelling long-term with kids. Slowly but surely, it dawned on us that with a little bit of luck and a lot of courage we *could* really make it happen. We *could* take a year out of our normal lives. One very influential factor for us was that Tim's employer, the police force, does allow officers to apply for a career break of up to a year for 'reasons of personal improvement'. Although Tim's employment as a police officer, day to day, was a major source of stress and negativity, we had now found a redeeming feature in being part of such a huge organisation. This option was a major factor in us making the decision to go for it. The safety net of knowing that Tim could walk back into a secure job once we returned from our travels, of course, made the decision considerably easier for us than it would be for the majority of families whose employers don't offer such an opportunity. Tim filled in the necessary paperwork, we crossed our fingers, and we were amazed and terrified in equal measure when his request was granted.

By this point we had spent many evenings scouring the internet for inspiration and had discovered that, in fact, there were other families out there, travelling long term and home-schooling their children. Seeing photos and posts from families like lifeinourvan and lulalastic on Instagram and Facebook encouraged me to start seeing this pipe-dream as a possible reality. It also made us realise that buying a campervan was the way to go. Breaking down the details, Tim and I had worked out that to make it feasible we needed to travel from September to August. This would minimise the disruption to the kids' schooling and would allow me to both finish a school teaching year and be back again to start a new one. Our youngest was due to start school in 2017 so we could apply for his school place in September before we left the UK and then send him off in his uniform when we got back. I might be a dreamer but I am also the organised, logistics girl when I need to be. I had made colour-coded charts and mapped it all out. It was totally possible. Sounds simple, right?

Our planning and scheming had also made one thing very clear.

It was going to cost a lot of money. Motorhomes are expensive, fuel is expensive, travelling is expensive and our pounds were suddenly worth far fewer Euros than they had been pre-Brexit. Not that we had many pounds anyway. I don't think we can be alone in having no savings? For many years we had been living pay cheque to pay cheque, occasionally putting emergency purchases on the credit card or re-mortgaging the house and increasing our debts. Needed a new boiler? We just put the mortgage term back up to 30 years *again*. Three pairs of new school shoes and two pairs of football boots required? Time to call on the old friend Credit Card! Don't get me wrong, in no way could we count ourselves as poverty stricken- we both worked in professional capacities and had decent enough salaries-but we certainly didn't feel rich and we never, ever had any money left at the end of the month. We were permanently chasing our own financial tail.

Having had the estate agents round to discuss the possibilities of renting or selling the house, and having spoken to the mortgage company, another thing was obvious- we were going to have to sell the house to finance the trip. We were so set on the idea by now that although we loved our house (and had spent a lot of time and money on making it beautiful), we were prepared to sell it to make this dream a reality. However, it was already April and we needed to leave by September. And there was a post-Brexit slump in the housing market. We were only going to get one shot at this. It wasn't going to be plain sailing. There were a lot of things that could go wrong.

TELLING PEOPLE

Breaking the news of our plans to the rest of the world presented us with us with our first major challenge. At this point, we had still not let anyone else in on our idea. I am aware that I have a reputation of being a bit flighty and I didn't want to end up with egg on my face if another one of my plans came to nothing. We also were anticipating some hostile reactions from some of the family and we didn't want to cause anyone any unnecessary stress. We hadn't even told the kids yet; we felt that there was no point exciting or worrying them if there was a chance it might not all fall into place. With this in mind, we put the house on the market but asked the estate agent NOT to put a 'For Sale' board up in the front garden. We hoped we could sell the house without needing one. What could possibly go wrong? Maybe if you have ever dealt with an estate agent you may have guessed where the weak link in our plan was?! Returning home from an impossibly stressful after-school marathon of multiple swimming lessons, car-picnic-teas plus Cub Scouts, with a car full of tired children I pulled onto my drive to find, of course, a glaring FOR SALE sign erected for all to see. We lived in a small town. The sign had been up for hours. Our secret was out.

After calming down the confused children and venting more than a little steam down the phone to the estate agent, I realised the game was up. We had to call our parents and tell them what was going on before they found out from someone else.

I think Tim and I played rock, paper, scissors to see who had to go first. Making these phone calls was something we had worried about ever since we took our first steps down this path of dreams. It was hard to imagine what our parents were going to think but we thought that Tim's dad would be the most concerned. Unluckily for Tim, his paper was beaten by my scissors and he had to go first. Tim's dad, a police officer himself for thirty years, is a wonderful man. He is also a sensible and sage man, fond of planning, preparing and sticking at things. He is not a quitter and not prone to wild bouts of spontaneity. We expected caution and concern. We had underestimated him. What we got was kindness and open-mindedness. He didn't tell us we were mad at all. Instead he offered us some money to help us on our way! We couldn't believe our luck! We rather rushed into the next phone calls thinking they would all be as easy as that one. My dad, as predicted, was typically philosophical, praising our vision, gently encouraging caution with the overall message to "trust our instincts and-as long as we were ABSOLUTELY sure we were doing the right thing-then go for it". More sighs of relief. There was only my mum left to tell and I thought I could absolutely handle it. My mum is a woman who has always flown in the face of convention so I thought she would praise our sense of adventure and admire our courage. I was wrong. Telling Mum was really hard. She was heartbroken. I hadn't really thought about the impact our trip would have on the rest of the family. I'd been too worried about the five of us. When we had been deliberating about whether or not we could really go for it, we had figured that as all our parents are in good health we should seize our opportunity to escape while they didn't need us. Aware that they might need more care from us in years to come, we thought we should make the most of our freedom and grab our adventure whilst we could. Unexpectedly though, it turned out Mum did need us. She needed cuddles and puzzles and ice-creams with her grandchildren more than I had realised. Making my mum cry was the first point at which I really took a deep breath and wondered if we were doing the right thing.

WITH THE CAREER BREAK APPROVED, the house on the market, our parents informed and local friends asking questions, the next step was to talk to our children. The kids were aged 8, 6 and 3 at this point. To ease them in, one weekend we took them to the local motorhome dealership and let them have fun looking inside all the vans- climbing into bunkbeds and exploring all the tiny kitchens etc. We told them we were thinking about buying a van and going travelling for the summer holidays. They thought this sounded like a brilliant idea. We let this notion settle in their minds for a while.

Having been blessed with three healthy, energetic, fun-loving kids, our gut instinct was that they would gain so much from the opportunities that would arise whilst travelling. They were at the heart of our dream. We envisaged visiting cool, historical sites with them; spending lots of time outdoors; learning snippets of new languages; trying new foods; experiencing other cultures and doing plenty of home-schooling to keep their brains ticking over. What made us nervous was that the older two loved school. They had nice friends and are the kind of children who love learning. They were also active members of scout groups and football teams. I wondered how they would feel about leaving all of that behind for a year. I needed to present the plan in the most positive way possible. Bribery was (as usual) a big part of my plan.

I let their Dad collect them from school and I left a treasure hunt in the house, instructing them to change clothes and meet the youngest and me in the local coffee shop. Once they arrived there I presented them each with their favourite magazine and let them choose any cake and drink they liked (they were onto me by this point, this NEVER normally happens!). This was *reckless* expenditure! Once they had filled their faces with overpriced chocolate treats we took a deep breath and reminded them about the plan we'd discussed for a summer holiday in a motorhome. We explained that, in fact, we wanted to see more of Europe than we could see in just six weeks and wondered how they would feel about going away for a bit longer. Maybe a year. The sugar rush paid off and they were all jumping about with excitement. So far so good.

"But, it's a big step and you've probably got some questions about it," we added gently. And over the course of an hour or so we tried to excite and reassure them, in equal measure. They had some excellent questions:

"What about school?"

"What about Christmas?"

"how many toys can we take?"

and some thoughtful observations:

"I think I'll miss my friends,"

"I feel sad about selling the house,"

"It will be strange not to see our grandparents for a year."

Tim and I did our best to listen to their concerns and answer their worries in the best way we could. We explained that yes, Christmas would be different this year, but that Santa *would* still find them. Yes, it would be sad to say goodbye to the house but the van would be our home and as long as we were all together, wherever we lived would feel like our home. We talked about the fact that they often reported being bored at school because the work was too easy and explained that I could make special lessons at just the right level for them. We gave them a funky notepad with different sections. We told them they could write down any more questions in it for us to talk about at another time, or if they had any worries, they could write them in there too. There was also a section for them to write down any ideas they had for the trip; things that they'd like to do or see. Over the next few weeks, it was this section that filled up the quickest-

"I'd like to see the Eiffel Tower,"

"I want to try tapas in Spain,"

"I want to learn to speak Spanish,"

"I want to play football with Daddy every day,"

and in the tricky times it was this excitement that allowed us to stay motivated and make it happen.

TELLING everybody else in our lives seemed to take on a weird trajectory. You imagine telling people in the order of their significance in your life but it doesn't work that way, of course. You tell the people you talk to first and before too long, you realise your oldest and most favourite friends are still in the dark. We found ourselves doing a lot of justifying. The most common reaction was "really?", followed by "you're brave!" and a significant number of "I wish I had the guts to do that!" These all sound, on the surface, quite supportive but the general, unspoken undertone was 'my god- you are completely crazy!' We also faced a lot of "God, are you sure you can't just rent your house out?" Selling the house seemed to be the maddest part to most people's minds. I don't know whether that's our British obsession with staying on the housing ladder or people's fears that without a base we wouldn't come back. I guess lots of people also knew how much time and money we had spent on improving our house and making it beautiful. It was true, we loved that house but in our recent deeper conversations we had come to realise that it was *just* a house and the truth was we were stuck in a spiral of constantly over-stretching ourselves financially, to try and afford making it just a little bit better. In the end, the house was likely to sink us. We had made our minds up; we didn't need the house, we needed the adventure. We had to sell it and we had to do it fast!

As you may well know, tidying your house up for viewings when you are trying to sell it is exhausting. Trying to do it when you have three young kids around is pretty close to impossible. We had lots of viewings but no bites. Perhaps it was the fact that the toilet-training-son kept pooing into the potty (or other non-sanctioned location) whenever anyone arrived? Perhaps it was the overwhelming number of Lego pieces tucked into every corner and crevice? Perhaps it was the oncoming house-price-crash the newspapers were predicting? We were getting frantic. In desperation we started looking into the possibility of appeasing all those soothsayers and renting the place out; we figured we could go away for just a few months and buy a beaten up old campervan. It would be a different trip than the one we'd envisaged but it would still be a big adventure. One thing was certain, we weren't going to give up on this dream too easily. At the final hour, an offer came in that was exactly what we needed. The SOLD sign was up and there was no looking back.

DECONSTRUCTING A LIFE

So, we would be moving out of our five bedroomed house very soon. We would be moving into a very small motorhome and packing all our remaining worldly goods into a single, rented garage. We needed to downsize. Big-time.

Slowly, but surely, I began getting rid of the mountains and mountains of *stuff* that our house was filled with. Toys, clothes, coats, shoes, furniture, board-games, books, bikes...endless box-loads of it. It was shipped off to friends with younger children, donated to charity, sold on and recycled. It seemed never-ending. How, I asked myself, had we accumulated so much?

I can't pretend it was an easy process. I cannot claim to have been instantly liberated from consumerism by relinquishing my worldly goods. But, do you know what, the more that went, the more I realised how little we actually needed in our lives. At first, I felt pangs of grief when I thought about selling the play-kitchen that had been a major feature of our playroom since my daughter was born. For almost seven years that hideously expensive wooden kitchen had been played with every single day. I freely admit that I felt crushed as its new owner took it away.

Then there were the trendy Swedish high chairs- almost nine years we'd had the eldest's one. Would we cope without them I wondered? Could I bear to let them go? They went. I felt OK about it; there was more space at the table and the kids didn't even notice.

Then there were the Toy Story toys, the dressing up costumes I had photographed them in with their cousins when they were tiny, the baby clothes I had saved 'just in case' another baby came along, the cot... Before too long, it was all gone. And rather than the absence I had feared, I did start to feel truly liberated and cleansed by the process.

Take cosmetics for instance. I don't call myself a glamour-puss, I don't lust after the latest make-up and bubble bath, yet still I had a MOUNTAIN of the stuff stashed here, there and everywhere. Moving into the van meant I could take one moisturiser, one deodorant, one shampoo and one hairbrush. I shudder to think of the value of the stuff I threw away. Neglected, unwarranted, unused. I survived for a year with the handful of toiletries that fitted into one small washbag. When I finished one, I replaced it. But not before. Not because they were on special offer. Not because I saw the advert and thought it looked nice. For a year, I just bought what I *needed* and nothing more. And did I look (or smell) any different for it? Nope. Not a jot. By the end of the trip I was struggling to remember what any of that stuff other stuff could have possibly been. I even went to TWO weddings during our year of adventure and I STILL didn't buy any extra cosmetics. And do you know what? I look better in the photos from those weddings than I ever did in any of the wedding pics for which I had primed and preened and made myself up to the nines with some new special make-up products bought just for the occasion. It seems that maybe happiness (and a touch of sunshine) is the best possible make-over tool!

And how did the kids take this annihilation of their toy collection? Well, at first there were some stricken faces at the prospect of giving away their possessions. But, as with most things, they soon got on board with the idea. Any money we made went into their 'Fun Fund'- a stash of cash for them to spend during our trip on adventures and activities of their own choosing. A different kind of 'stuff', which would prove to be much more valuable to them than the bits we had sold: they bought ice-creams on the beach, a kayaking trip on a Spanish river, packets of sweets in the Christmas markets, a session of ice-skating... stuff that their Mum can never sell and that won't gather dust. It occurs to me now, that we had already started educating them into the different kind of life we had envisaged, before we had even departed the UK. They (and I) realised pretty quickly that this was all just *stuff*. And none of it really mattered very much. Seeing the collaborative skills they needed to negotiate the spending of the fun-fund was a joy to witness. As were their faces as they experienced these little luxuries that they had bought for themselves. We went from having a sizeable house, jam packed full of toys to having one small box of Lego and one small tub of 'other' toys. This was sufficient to last them a year and I have never known my children to play in such imaginative and collaborative ways as they did on our adventure. We have all vowed to never let the volume of toys get so out of control again. They even began planning what else they would give away or sell once we got back home!

Until we embarked on this journey, too much of our lives had been taken up with hankering for, obtaining and paying-off-the-debts for more *stuff*. It turns out, we were much better off without it.

SAYING GOODBYE

Everyone hates goodbyes don't they? Leaving the people you love- whether it is for a few hours when you leave the kids crying at nursery; or for a few weeks when you kiss goodbye to the parents who live further away than you'd like; or even for a year as you head off on a very big adventure- is never easy.

The week that our adventure began saw us saying goodbye to some utterly fabulous people. As a woman with, at the best of times, the emotional stability of a hormonal blancmange, this was something I found really difficult. Photographic evidence proves that I got progressively redder and blotchier as the goodbyes wore on. I managed to hold it together as I left my farewell dinner with my oldest school friends (having to run for the train helped!). Tears did begin to well as I watched my son's emotional goodbye to his school friends and his last goal for his football club, but my cheeks were still (largely) tear free. Leaving the house we had raised our children in for six years was a wrench and I shed a fair few tears as I reminisced over the happy memories we had made there. But that was nothing compared to the final few days full of brilliant friends and family who kept surprising us with thoughtful gifts and farewell parties. Friends cried and then I bawled. My sister couldn't look me in the eye so we hugged and blubbed. My dear old mum (from whom I get the teary-genes) was beside herself and I matched her sobs with my own (especially when I read her lovely card). It was a train-wreck!

But as we drove away in the van and the fug of emotion lifted, I came to realise that actually, it had been the most wonderful week. I had spent the kind of time with my friends and family that we can never normally seem to fit in. We had BBQs with good people, ate hotdogs and played in the forest with friends, spent time drinking and laughing with my sisters, let the kids stay up late playing with their cousins, took my Dad to the zoo, celebrated in restaurants with all the family... Basically we made time for all those people that we normally neglect because we are too busy dragging our kids to parties they'd rather avoid, tearing our hair out in queues at DIY shops and supermarkets or attending events we feel we *ought* to attend but don't really enjoy. In fact, I can't tell you what a relief it was to eschew all those drudgeries for a while and just spend time with the people we love the most. Not only that, but we spoke aloud our feelings and told people what they really mean to us. So, in-all, I came to thinking that maybe goodbyes aren't such a bad thing after all.

With the wind tearing through our hair as we stood on the deck of the ferry and waved goodbye to the white cliffs, I was struck by the idea that we are, of course, all heading towards our one unavoidable and very final goodbye. I fear that, all too often, we save expressing our feelings for what we imagine will be our final precious moments with a person. In my experience though we end up only saying these words at that person's funeral because we missed our chance. In recent years, the universe has been sending us some clanging reminders that life is brutally short. That's part of what inspired our big adventure and our reason for embracing this gift of time with our children. From now on, I plan to embrace the goodbye and see it for what it is- a chance to tell people that we love them. Don't underestimate the power of a good goodbye!

REALITY HITS HOME

A couple of my favourite friends laid bets that I would return from this trip pregnant. Although they did not get to cash in any winnings, babies were certainly on my mind during the first few weeks of the trip. As we set off into Europe, in the van we knew very little about, I came to dwell on the similarities between motor homing and those dark, beautiful early days of parenthood. There were a number of points of comparison:

1. When you become a parent, there is a sudden moment of realisation that your life will never be the same again. It hits you like a fist in the throat. Driving off the ferry, on the wrong side of the road in a beast of a van that we had no idea how to use gave us that feeling in spades. We now had no house, no jobs, no school

places, no route planned out and very little idea what we were doing! There really was no turning back.

2. When you become a parent you feel you have been thrown, head-first into a universe that you don't understand and don't have the skills to navigate. Instead, you have to learn them by making mistake after mistake. "Silly you!" the midwife clucks, "of course you can't cut a baby's nails with baby-nail-clippers!". The motor homing equivalent of that is the mean French driver who beeps and makes rude gestures as you try to reverse your stupidly tall vehicle back from the supermarket entrance height-barrier. Or the campsite owner who angrily explains that you can only hang your washing in the designated areas. Or the Dutch couple laughing at you as you tip your pasta on the floor whilst trying to drain it through a kids' beach-sieve...
3. Once you've given birth, your tiny little baby means that leaving your house becomes the most challenging mission you have ever undertaken. Suddenly, getting beyond your front door takes several hours and is impossible before 11am because there are a million considerations and things to pack that you had never had to think of before. Milk, wet wipes, muslins, change of clothes, toys, snacks, breast pads...etc etc. Living in a motorhome creates a very similar problem! You have to pack everything, and I mean *everything*, into a cupboard (and there are only 5 of these) before you go anywhere. If you fail to do so, your things will spin wildly, like missiles, off whatever surface they were left on and hit your children on the head. "AVALANCHE!" was a cry we heard from the back quite a lot in the first few weeks as the granola box

overturned once *again*, sprinkling sugary oats all over the children. Then there's the fact that anything metal needs to be wrapped up in case of desperately loud rattles. You also need to wind in all the windows you opened because it's so bloody hot trying to sleep in a tin van. You need to fill the water, empty the toilet, unplug the electric... honestly- it's a marathon!

4. Then there's the poo. Oh, the world of learning there is to do about poo, both when welcoming a tiny baby-poo-machine into the world and when learning to use a motorhome's cassette toilet. This was a true baptism of fire. Luckily for me, Tim took the lead on this and I only ever emptied the toilet ONCE on the whole trip! (I figure it's the least he could do to repay me for all those years I spent breastfeeding!)

All this said, we quickly realised that motor homing is wonderful. Really wonderful. By the time we'd reached Spain, we were in love with a new lifestyle. At a gorgeous campsite called 'La Paz' in the Asturias, we were perched on an incredible cliff-side pitch. We could eat all three meals looking out across the most beautiful bay and we were lulled to sleep every night by the sound of the waves tickling the beach. I mean, seriously, these kinds of views in a hotel room would cost you a small fortune. We could pootle down to the sandy cove in under five minutes and there we could swim, build sandcastles and hold' beach olympics' to our hearts' content. Not only that, but there was a little bar on site, serving fresh tapas and gloriously cheap Riojas , where we sat, playing cards and thanking our lucky stars as they shone over the ocean in front of us. It sounds idyllic. It really was.

The first leg of our journey, along the Northern coast of Spain from San Sebastian (amazing) to Santiago de Compostella (spectacular) was the perfect place to begin our tour. All along this coast we stopped in the most jaw-droppingly beautiful places and called them our home. It is an area we had never considered for a holiday before and we instantly fell in love with the passion of the place. The landscape, for one thing, was amazing. There are a series of mountains there-The Picos De Europa-which took our breath away. We had expected Spain to show us a rather rugged, arid landscape. We couldn't have been more wrong. Driving through the Picos, we were surrounded by lush, verdant hills and mountains, rich with wildlife and water features. And less than an hour's drive from the mountains you find windswept, endlessly sandy beaches which we often had all to ourselves. The locals are justifiably proud of the distinctive music of the Asturias and Galicia-which is heavily influenced by Celtics roots. Its sound is haunting and powerful and to sit listening to it on a warm evening, with a local cider in your hand is something close to heavenly. We never wanted to leave. Even the menus, which are the same, *exactly the same,* in every single bar or restaurant you visit (because this is the Galician food and *why* would anyone consider *ever* eating anything else?!) didn't get us down. Although the paprika flavoured octopus on mashed potato might not be everyone's cup of tea, Northern Spain welcomed us with open arms and we fell deeply in love with it.

However, if I return to my metaphor for a moment, there was also a darker side to our early days on the road. Like that newborn baby, there were things, at first, that kept us awake at night and scared the living daylights out of me. Campsites are amazing. But campsites are expensive. They also close at the end of the season and the holiday makers had all gone home by this point at the end of September. So we had to do a spot of what motorhomers call 'wild camping'. In essence, it means sleeping somewhere which isn't a designated campsite or resting place. It's a grey legal area in Spain, although our books and chatrooms told us it is largely tolerated in these areas, it took me a while to get used to it. Sharing a beach car park with bunch of surfers and hippies felt very odd at first and it was a while before I stopped dreaming about being woken up by the furious bangs of marauding thieves or angry Guardia Civil.

There was definitely a settling in period which we spent simultaneously grieving the loss of our old home comforts and rejoicing in our new found freedoms. Here is an overview of the pros and cons as we saw them in those first few weeks:

PRO: We got to live wherever we liked. Sea views like that would cost mega-money any other way. With a motorhome they cost about £22 per night.

CON: Sometimes we had to live in yucky car-parks en-route to the beautiful places. At such times, I slept with the frying pan by my side in case of intruders!

PRO: We had begun to live a very outdoor lifestyle which was fab. Lots of walking, playing, cycling and swimming.
CON: Outdoor life= mucky kids and wet swimming stuff. Nothing dries in a motorhome. Ever.

PRO: The children were staying up so late and getting so much fresh air that they were enjoying lie-ins until 8:30/9am every day.
CON: (There were no downsides to this. Every day, for nine years, at least one of the children had, unfailingly, been awake before 6:30am. Family lie-ins were a total joy!)

PRO: There was often no wi-fi. Freedom from all those distractions and nonsense was a very beautiful thing!
CON: There was often no wi-fi. Sometimes you just need that Facebook hit/Peppa Pig episode.

PRO: All the clothes I had for a whole year fitted into one tiny holdall and I hadn't worn make-up for weeks. This was quite liberating.
CON: This was also quite stinky and occasionally my eyebrows took over my face!

PRO:We all ate together, every meal time and the hungry children were trying and enjoying new foods.
CON: Three tiny hob rings and the world's smallest oven were never going to satisfy my culinary ambitions.I missed my Kitchenaid!

PRO: I could hear all my children breathing while they slept. I found this utterly enchanting and reassuring.
CON: Bedroom privacy in a motorhome is essentially a very

thin curtain. There would be very little chance of making that fourth baby!

STEEP though the learning curve was, I did take heart from looking back at how we had struggled out of those first weeks of being parents and how much easier everything had got over time. I held out hope that before long, Tim and I would be masters of the whole motor-homing affair. We too would soon be smiling wryly at those other novices around us as *they* struggled to connect the water tap/pay the tolls/negotiate the levelling chocks/fill up with autogas etc. After all, we had eventually reached the point where we *could* now manage to bundle three small kids out of the house, all dressed, with clean teeth, healthy packed lunches, brushed hair, PE kits and reading books AND get them to school by 8:30am! Well, we used to anyway... on the road at that hour in the morning we were only just opening the curtains and smiling at the waves!

CHAPTER 2

OUR ROUTE AROUND EUROPE

"Where did you go?"

Having waved goodbye to our lives, we drove off the ferry in France with very little idea of where we were going and what we would do when we got there. In the final weeks before departure, people kept saying to me "oh you must have done a lot of planning?" This struck fear into my heart. The truth was that we had been so busy getting the *ending* of everything sorted out (getting the house sold, getting rid of all our stuff, purchasing the van, saying goodbye to everyone etc.) that there had been minimal time to look ahead and give any thought to our trip! We had hastily ordered a road map of Spain and a book of aires and campsites we could stay in but the books still lay in the cardboard packaging they had arrived in, and beyond that we really had nothing. We knew we wanted to get down to Spain as quickly as possible to try and find some good weather before winter set in, but we had very little clue of what to do beyond putting 'Spain' into the Sat Nav. So that's what we did. We flew through France at break-neck speed, with our eyes on the prize- España. Unfortunately, a little planning would have prepared us for the fact that the tolls on French motorways are ENORMOUS. We were spending over €100 a day on tolls, one road alone cost us €80. Eighty Euros into ONE toll machine?! This was a painful lesson learned. When we returned to France later in the trip, we took all the slow roads and what a joy it was to see the beautiful countryside, stop at the world class local-bakers and not have to pay out for any tolls. But, like I said, back at the start of our trip we were the greenest novices the motor-homing world has ever seen! By the time we got to Bordeaux we'd had enough. The kids had had enough. We had gone from big smiles on the ferry to tears and tantrums in the backseat in the space of 48 hours. We'd promised our kids a big adventure and all they'd had so far was motorways and long driving days. We noticed signs for a campsite. Finally giving in to the squabbling and moaning emanating from the rear of the van, we pulled over and checked it out. It was called 'Dune de Pilat' and the sign said it had a pool, a play area, football pitch and lots of sand. We couldn't drive another mile. The decision was easy-we were going to bed down for a few days and properly start our adventure. This was the start of a new style of decision making for us. It was such a change from the carefully thought-out, planned and executed lifestyle we had lived back in the UK. It was an absolute breath of fresh air to just free-wheel for a while. We soon discovered that planning was for the other life. This trip was all about making it up as we went along!

Dune de Pilat turned out to be a major highlight of the trip. We found out that this is the tallest sand dune in Europe It is hugged on all sides by sea or pine forest. We had an absolute whale of a time clambering up it and then rolling, sausage-roll style back down again. That first night, the five of us sat right at the top, watching paragliders running off the edge of the dunes then dancing around in the air. Witnessing their visible sense of freedom as they took that leap, we smiled as we realised that this was an uncanny metaphor for our own big leap. Looking over at our children, happy as anything to be off the leash and sitting miles away from us, sharing their own gorgeous sunset together, we felt as though we were in the middle of another world. Up there, with the kids nowhere near bed, not worrying about homework or club-pick-ups or tea-time-it not only *felt* different but everything *looked* different too. I felt a bit like I was in a desert. All we could see for miles around was sand and sky. It was a totally magical experience. And at that moment it finally hit me. We had done it. We had escaped the rat race and all the pressures that come with 'normality'. We had really leapt off the edge of life. I welled up with pride and wonder at that moment and all my worries fell away. I knew we were going to be OK.

Later that night, as we walked back though the luscious-smelling pine trees, singing and skipping along together, we bumped into another family of five who also happened to be talking English so we got chatting. Just a moment before, we had sat feeling like the most courageous adventurers in the world and here we were, confronted with another family who had done *exactly* the same thing *us!* The Brave-Brighton family had upped sticks, sold their home and moved into a camper van just like us. They had even left the UK the same day we had. It was the most bizarre coincidence. We invited them over for a few beers and the children ran off to enjoy their newfound friends and freedom, running through the forest and whooping with delight. The grown-ups sat back and revelled in the gleeful lack of bedtime routine, watching the kids' head torch beams bounce around under that gorgeous night sky whilst we enjoyed a long chat with our new friends. It didn't take us long to work out that Justin and Tams are awesome. Over the next few days we all struck up a very beautiful friendship. It wasn't to be the last we saw of the Brave-Brightons!

That experience: happening upon an incredible place, exactly the kind of thing we hoped to show our children- something wondrous and different and awe-inspiring, gave us the courage to know we were doing the right thing. And it happened time and time again in our year abroad. Of course there were things and places that we had planned to see; landmarks like The Eiffel Tower, The Colosseum, The Leaning Tower of Pisa, Legoland etc were never going to be missed off our agenda and many of those blew our minds too, but these other, unexpected places that we found by chance or because of a quick chat with a smiling stranger, these were the places and experiences that really changed our lives in a pretty significant way during our big adventure.

There were also some moments of bewildering good fortune. One particularly poor session of map-reading on my part led us to be utterly lost in Germany one day and teetering on the edge of a blazing row. But we suddenly heard a roar of engines and saw the entrance to the Nürburgring (the world-famous motor-sports complex)! It was never on our radar as a place to visit, we had no idea that we were anywhere near it, but we'd seen it on Top Gear and heard about it from petrol-head friends. So we pulled over, parked for free, walked in and watched some very cool and very fast cars whizz around the ring at top speed. We even watch a helicopter take off. It was a brilliant bit of impromptu entertainment that made us the envy of a lot of people on social media and it was a total fluke.

Another time that the road led us in the right direction was when we were fighting with Italy. We had found the whole country hard-going in so many ways and although we had loosely planned to spend 2 months there, after 6 weeks, we had had enough. We'd decided to spend a few days driving up the Eastern side, quickly visiting Venice before legging it out of the country and heading into Slovenia. However, Italy had other plans for us. One fateful day, every single place we tried to stop turned out to be derelict or closed or impossible to find or full of dodgy looking ne'er-do-wells. Honestly, we were at the end of our tether. That day we just kept driving, and driving, and driving. The kids were wailing from the back "but you promised we'd stop in an hour and it's been FOUR HOURS!"

"We're so sorry!" we'd weep from the front. "We did TRY to stop but we can't find anywhere to park/there was a team of very suspicious-looking men prowling around the van/(and then later) the bl**dy campsite has shut down/(and subsequently) the road doesn't exist..." Of all the days that stick in my mind as being a point when we *considered* giving up on our adventure entirely, this was the worst. In the end, we found ourselves on the motorway again, after seven hours of driving and we seemed to be heading straight for Venice. Tim and I turned to each other and said "Let's just see Venice and then get the hell out of this country!"

So we got to Venice about four days earlier than we had planned and our love affair with Italy was well and truly over. But not for long. Italy will do that to you! Having negotiated the bus into Venice, we fought our way onto the boat taxi and sat, exhausted, hoping that the rain would stop soon. But the trip threw us another curve-ball. One by one, people started getting onto the water taxi in masks. You know, the kind you see people wearing for masked balls. My daughter poked me in the ribs and pointed. This was cool! We were smiling again. Then more people got on, these guys were wearing costumes too. Then more people. The further we got towards the city centre, the bigger the costumes became and by the end of it I was unashamedly up on my feet taking photos of Venetians dressed in the most elaborate and beautiful costumes I had ever seen. Looking out of the window at the gondoliers and iconic striped poles I had only ever seen in the movies, surrounded by these wonderful colours and creations, I felt like I was in the most surreal dream of my life. Well, we got off the boat at St Mark's square and realised that we were in the middle of carnival.

Venice 'Carnivale' is incredible and we had stumbled upon it, by chance, because of some bad campsites and terrible Italian roads. It was one of the happiest accidents of my life and I could not stop smiling. We got absolutely wrapped up in this amazing festival. Literally everywhere we turned, there were Venetian Carnival-goers preening their feathers and posing for photos, strutting down the stages and we even got to see 'the flight of an angel' where a young girl is launched on a huge zip-wire across the square from the top of the tower. It was such an exhilarating, surreal occasion that we bought ourselves some traditional masks and spent the day wandering this beautiful town, seeing everything through new, masked, eyes. We ate the world's finest pizza sitting on the street corner followed by incredible fritadella (little fried doughnuts flavoured in a variety of ways) and felt as though we had walked straight into a dream. The truth is, had we done more research and known carnival was happening, we most likely would have avoided it, imagining that we wouldn't get a campsite and the roads would be gridlocked etc. Our total lack of planning led us to one of the most magical moments of the trip (and of my life). Seriously, if you ever get the opportunity, visit Venice at Carnival time. Its out of this world!

Our big year abroad was an incredible lesson for us all that life will show you some wonderful things if you just let it. It will bring you cool people, beautiful places, fun experiences and a wealth of adventure if you can just stop planning and start exploring.

And so, with very little planning and lots of perfect accidents (plus more than a few pitfalls) we made our way across the continent, stopping in at 19 countries along the way. Our grand tour of Europe took us through:

- France
- Spain

- Portugal
- Monaco
- San Marino
- Italy
- The Vatican City
- Slovenia
- Croatia
- Bosnia
- Austria
- Luxemburg
- Hungary
- Czech Republic
- Germany
- Sweden
- Denmark
- Belgium
- The Netherlands

North Sea
United Kingdom
Denmark
Ireland
Netherlands
Poland
London
Berlin
Germany
Belgium
Prague
Paris
Czechia
Vienna
Slovakia
Austria
France
Hungary
Croatia
Serbia
Italy
Barcelona
Rome
Portugal
Madrid
Spain
Google
Map data ©2018 Google, ORION-ME
© Scribble Maps

CHAPTER 3

ROAD-SCHOOLING

"So what did you do about school?"

***Homeschooling and the law- The nitty gritty**:*

In the UK, any parent has the right to homeschool their child. You do not have to be a teacher, or undertake any training. You simply write to your child's school and notify them of your intentions. If you child has not yet entered school then you can notify the local council. The local council 'can' make an informal enquiry to see if they think your child is receiving a decent education, but my reading and anecdotal evidence suggest that very little monitoring is undertaken by Local Authorities (who are stretched enough as it is). Home Educators are not obliged to agree to home visits unless in rare or extreme circumstances. Laws can be very different in other countries. For example, in Sweden, Croatia, and Germany, homeschooling is illegal and in Switzerland and many other countries, it is only allowed under very restrictive and strict guidelines.

Most people are surprised to hear how easy it was to remove our children from school and how little support or questioning we received from the authorities. Personally, I found this to be a very positive thing and I can see that there really is not the manpower or incentive for Local Authorities to get involved in such a minority of children's lives unless they are brought to the attention of Social Services through other means.

---

* * *

I AM A TEACHER. I became a teacher straight out of university so I am your quintessentially institutionalised educationalist. Basically, I have spent my entire life in schools. So, you might surmise, it was a big step to take my children out of school for a year. And no, the school didn't offer to hold their places open or hand us any nicely organised teaching resources; it was up to us and we were all on our own. The older two, at the time of leaving, were 6 and 8 years old. Both smart, both liked school. I think a lot of people found this aspect of our trip, the hardest to understand. Why would I take such a risk with my children's education? Wouldn't they be horribly behind when we got back? A year later, I can promise you that this couldn't be further from the truth. Here's a little insight into how Road-schooling benefited our children:

THE FIRST COUNTRY we visited for any length of time was Spain. Travelling in Spain, in October, we found ourselves amongst a swathe of silver-surfers: retired motor homers who, en-masse, head to the southern sunshine for the winter. Often, in those first few months, our arrival must have reduced the average age on a campsite by about forty years! It is hard to go un-noticed in such circumstances, particularly when you have brought three noisy children into the mix to ruin everyone's peaceful retirement sunsets. On the whole, people were very amenable and would often stop and chat with us. More than once, the kids were given sweets by a kind, bronzed older lady and to our relief most people said they were amazed by how well our kids played together (this was something we had noticed too- suddenly our kids seemed much more of a team). Occasionally though, we did see a couple glance at each other with fear in their eyes as we arrived on the adjacent pitch to them. I also think there were a few times when we hastened the departure of a some campers who felt they might just move on down the coast a little quicker than expected! Still, we did find that one advantage of noisy kids was securing yourself a bit of a wide berth!

Anyway, in our chats with the less grumpy aged adventurers, one of the first things they always wanted to know was what we were doing about school. There had been a lot in the British press at the time about a father taking his case to the Supreme

Court because he had refused to pay a fine for taking his kids out of school for a two week holiday. And yet here we were, taking our kids out of school for A WHOLE YEAR! I think it would be fair to say that most people seemed a little incredulous of our reckless attitude to education until, that is, Tim usually found himself pointing out:

"My wife is a teacher," as a kind of self-justification. This almost always resulted in a big smile of relief from our fellow campers and a comment along the lines of "oh well then, you'll be fine!"

DO YOU NEED TO BE A TEACHER?

Whilst I do think there is some truth in the notion that my profession gave me the confidence to take my children out of school for a year, I think that in practice, very few of my teaching skills came into play in road-schooling our three. I am trained to teach English Literature to students aged 11-18. I am no expert in the curriculum of 3,6 and 8 year olds. I know a lot about Shakespeare's tragedies, Post-Colonial fiction and Metaphysical poetry. I know how to teach students to write a good essay and manage their time effectively. I do not know very much about the learning patterns of young children. Except that, of course, I do. I have been a parent to these young people from the second the gametes fused in my womb and there is no-one who knows them better than me. Looking back on the year, I think that the education our children received was an astounding success. But the success came from the adventure, the children themselves and us as parents, and I really don't think you need to be a teacher to enable this kind of learning to take place at all.

One of our most memorable early stops was at a tiny little village called Covodonga, up in the Picos De Europa mountains in the Asturias, Northern Spain. When my daughter is asked about the highlights of her trip, she still often recalls it as one of her favourite places to see. Now, this was probably ten days into our trip and we were very much finding our feet with the road-schooling. Tim and I had read up on the significance of the village and why it was a site of pilgrimage, but we were a bit nervous that the kids might not find it very interesting. Tim (not the teacher remember) thought that maybe we could write them a quick treasure hunt, based on what we'd researched. So, as the van wound its way up the impossibly steep mountain roads, we quickly scribbled down a few questions which we hoped might intrigue the children and lead them to discover the most interesting details of Covodonga. We gave it to the kids and told them there would be a prize if they could complete it as a team.

Clearly, this quiz was the most simple idea in the world. It took us about ten minutes' worth of effort but the impact it had on our family visit to Covodonga was amazing. The children were so excited to be in charge of the visit and so keen to find out more that they were literally dragging us away from our coffees in the bar so that they could visit the waterfall and see what happens if you drink some of the water from it. We were then pulled off to the chapel so they could find out who famously appeared there to which famous warrior. Please understand, these are normal kids; ordinarily, we are the ones dragging them to places of historical interest. It was so rewarding for us to watch them engage with the literacy, history, geography and culture with so little input from us.

Spanish legend has it that the Reconquista began in that tiny chapel in Covodonga, when The Madonna appeared to Don Pelayo (the great Spanish hero) as he prepared to fight back against the Moors and reclaim Spain on behalf of the Christians. In fairness, the story is a good one. There's the classic idea of a small hero, fighting back against a much stronger opposition and winning. But let's face it, if you had read it in a book at school, you'd forget it by the next day. However, by going there and seeing it, engaging with the history and touching it, I know my children will never forget that story or that place. And, as we roved across Spain, we kept finding statues of Don Pelayo or finding ourselves wandering down 'Rua Don Pelayo' and the kids would not only notice these details but retell this historical legend time and time again. It was learning that they could apply and see as relevant and that seemed to make an enormous difference to their interest, their memory and their retention of the details.

This kind of learning, the deeper understanding that they got from visiting places and learning things was played out hundreds of times, week after week as we made our way across this amazing continent full of history. Here are just a few examples:

RELIGIOUS EDUCATION:

In Santiago de Compostella, we followed the conch shells to the cathedral as the pilgrims have done for centuries. Then we sat looking at the huge fresco on the front of the cathedral, working out which biblical stories we could identify. Surrounded by pilgrims arriving, crying with happiness as they finished their epic journeys, my children will never forget what a pilgrimage is or why people might undertake one. They soon began to look, with interest, at stained glass windows, searching for a link to the natural imagery they had seen in the Sagrada Familia in Barcelona or the pictoral scenes of St Peter's Basilica in Rome. They came to understand that the iconography of a church is totally different to that of a mosque, because they visited the Mosque-Catherdral in Còrdoba, a mosque which had been taken over by the Christians and half converted into a Catholic church. They could see, side-by-side, the very different ways of decorating a sacred building. As they sat drawing the beautiful tessellated patterns they found in the Real Alcazar in Seville, these young children realised that there were no images of people or animals in Muslim buildings, just shapes, symmetry and clever uses of water and reflections. They asked me why this was so different to all the pictures and statues of people that we'd seen in all the churches we had visited. They worked these things out themselves and they remember it all now because they saw it everywhere we went.

ART AND CULTURE:

Whilst visiting Malaga, we chanced upon the wonderful Centre Pompdiou and the children could take part in a free activity about the artist Arman. They were hands on, sorting and collating and arranging and photographing. It was wonderful. At other times we did some watercolour paintings on the beach and learned to use oil pastels to imitate some of the Van Gogh artwork we saw in The Netherlands. Our eldest son went on a tour of The Vatican art gallery with a 'children's treasure hunt' audio guide which was an amazing way for him to find meaning amongst the huge collection of art there. He learned about a plethora of things from mummified remains through to Raphael then on to the stunning experience of standing in The Sistine Chapel and looking up to the visions of angels. Oh, and let's not forget the superb (and highly recommended) Children's Museum, Frida and Fred, in Graz, Austria, where they got to dress up as circus performers and take part in all kinds of circus events.

We had lots of opportunities for painting:

HISTORY:

History, of course, was everywhere, in every step we took, but some memorable examples were:

- at the castle built into the side of a Rock in Slovenia where we learned about sieges (and the weak spot where the king was finally killed- on the toilet!);
- visiting an underground Mausoleum for the early Christian dead in Porto;
- the epic splendour of the Colosseum and other Roman amphitheatres we found in Spain and Italy. We stopped to consider what the Gladiators must have endured there;
- Thinking long and hard about barriers and wondering what it must have felt like when the Berlin wall came down as we stood at Checkpoint Charlie;

- our morbid curiosity at the chapel made entirely from human bones in Faro;
- seeing the site where the civil war began in Croatia less than thirty years ago and the ruins of the tanks that had filled the streets there for four years. Not to mention marvelling at how well the country has repaired itself after such a bloody conflict.

One of our favourite road-schooling days was when we visited the working Viking centre in Ribe, Denmark (see more info in Section Ten). Here, we walked around a living re-created Viking village. As we entered the Jarl's longhouse, we were met by the Jarl's wife and the children were invited to dress up in traditional Viking costumes, feed the chickens, grind the flour, take part in traditional Viking games, make their own coins and see what kids' lives were like hundreds of years ago. The boys picked up some long sticks which were lying around and began sword fighting with them- the Viking lady fell about laughing before telling the boys that they "should be careful what they touch in here," because they were playing with bulls' penises! The boys quickly dropped them in disgust- another lesson learned! Enquiring as to why the Vikings kept bulls' penises in their homes, they found out that they were used for beating slaves. That was a lot to learn in five minutes! The kids were also taught to light fires with flints which became a skill they put to regular use for marshmallow toasting. The volunteers at the centre were in the process of recreating a Viking church and watching their exquisite method of carving took our breath away. A well as all this, the children took part in some warrior training and we learned all about the weapons the Viking warriors used and why they were effective. I cannot stress enough how much learning took place in just that one day. We learned, in a few hours, what would take weeks to get through in the classroom and all of it was so much more memorable and meaningful than it ever could have been from a book.

GEOGRAPHY:

I think that seeing such a variety of landscapes and covering such a large area of Europe has done wonders for everyone's geography. I can now point out countries on the map that I barely knew existed and after several hundred rounds of 'The Flag Game' I can now manage to recall a few European flags too (though not nearly as many as the kids!). Most people remember learning about volcanoes at school but how many children get to actually visit a volcanic crater? I know that, as a child, I learned about Pompeii in some boring Latin lessons at school but my children got to *actually go there!* We saw the fossilised forms of dogs and humans, stuck forever in their final gasps of terror when they were engulfed by molten lava and ash. We won't forget the eerie feel of all those streets which must have been alive with people one minute and filled with death the next. The site at Pompeii goes on for acres and the scale of devastation is quite overwhelming when you witness it for yourself, in the flesh.

LANGUAGES:

Ok, I'd be lying if I claimed we all came back having mastered a plethora of European languages. But the truth is that we learned a few words in every country we visited and in countries like Spain and France, where we stayed for longer periods, we did leave feeling that we could communicate at a basic level with a degree of success. At first, the children were very nervous about using the funny new words, but it was incredible to see how much their confidence grew as the trip progressed. By the time we reached France for the second time, they were begging to be allowed to go to the shop on their own in the mornings to order and buy the bread. They could confidently ask for "Deux pains s'il vous plait!" which brought them a great deal of pride. We all found out that a smile and some hand gestures will get you a long way and that having a go usually makes you very popular with your host. The kids struck up friendships with children when there was no common language besides Lego, football and toys. I remember them playing Uno for hours with a little German boy and innumerable games of football with a family of Swiss children. We had set out to show them that Europe was a place where people would work together in spite of their differences, and this was one really important road-schooling lesson.

One memorable lesson involved a treasure hunt around our French campsite. I sent the big two off to find a series of French words and phrases. They got to explore the campsite on their own (which they always love) and had to photograph the foreign words, in situ, and then guess their meaning. For example, they had to find the words 'salle de bains', take a photo of the sign and record what they thought the phrase meant (it's bathroom-if you're wondering!). The reason this was a brilliant lesson was that they were walking around reading all the French words they could see, developing their independence, and properly decoding a new language. It took me about 10 minutes to set it up, took them about an hour to compete and they absolutely loved it! I was asked to repeat the task several times! So much better than sitting at a textbook.

SCIENCE:

Whilst number one son was off enjoying the Vatican Art Gallery, the younger ones visited the truly wonderful science museum in Rome. Here they earned about healthy eating by shopping, stocking the shelves, and working on the tills in a miniature supermarket. They also drove a fire engine, powered a train with solar energy, learned about water pressure and a host of other hands' on experiences. There was another great science museum in Faro, Portugal, which had a brilliant little aquarium as part of it. We got to hold starfish and sea-slugs and all kind of wacky creatures. The children got to see, with their own eyes, how a starfish will regenerate itself when it loses a leg. We could see starfish with the stumps of new legs regrowing where the old leg had become detached and found out the the lost leg can even grow into a whole new starfish! There was also a fair amount of science in starting and maintaining camp-fires, flying kites, dissecting wild flowers, exploring rock pools and categorising living organisms on the beach.

Probably best of all was our trip to the 'Gelato University' just outside Bologna. Here we had a history lesson on the origins of gelato (it's not the same as ice-cream FYI) and the science behind getting a creamy texture, without crystals. Then we got to make our very own gelato as a family, hearing about the science of the fat-to-fruit ratios and the flavour combinations. Then we got to eat it. Lots of it. This was a very good day!

And then there was the Lindt chocolate museum in Cologne. Plenty of science (and eating) there too. We followed the process of chocolate making from bean to bar and learned all about the production and consumption of this beautiful product. We walked through a miniature rain forest and then saw the factory in motion, witnessing the end product arrive on the conveyor belt. That's my kind of science!

MATHS:

Easy. I mean, sure, I had a few Maths books with me and we did, sometimes, sit down to practise and develop Maths skills. But, there was also a lot of ad-hoc Maths learning going on by stealth. The children were very aware that we were working to a tight budget so they became much more conscious of how much things cost and how this varied from country to country. They also became dab hands at converting prices into Pound or Euros. We'd often ask them to pay for things in shops or cafes and ask them to work out the change. Then they had their 'Fun Fund' to negotiate spending. The 'Fun Fund' was the pot of money that we had accumulated from selling their toys etc before we left and it was a pot of cash for the kids to share. It was the only spending money we were giving them and it needed to last the entire trip. This resulted in some complex negotiating at times but all in the name of good Maths! They used it for ice-skating in Seville at the Christmas market, hiring go-karts in Denmark, and buying sweets and ice-creams when our family budget had run out.

(Also- see Section 7 'Money' for a real-life Maths lesson in Lidl!)

LITERACY:

So, this is my specialism. Until I left University I had spent my entire life with my head in a book. But somehow, since becoming a teacher and a mother, life had got in the way of reading. Of course I still found a few minutes in bed to read a Booker prize-winner here or there and I read the things I needed to teach, but I had spent far too little time on reading for many years. This was all to change on our big adventure. All of a sudden, free from the ceaseless distractions of wifi, work and TV, I was suddenly blessed with time to read. And as with most things, this became infectious. As the kids saw Tim and I reading, so they too picked up their books in quiet moments and we all read twenty times what we'd normally get through. One of the downsides to this was the cost! I realised how much of an asset a local library is to my normal life because all of a sudden I was having to BUY books. And sometimes the kids were getting through one a day! It was an element of trip expenditure that we had not anticipated or budgeted for. But what's money when your kids are reading, right? We made it a priority purchasing area and I'm glad we did.

In addition to private reading, we also found that we had more time and energy for reading with the older two at bedtimes and I picked more challenging titles than I had done in the past because I felt more able to deal with the complex questions and conversations that might arise from them. I enjoyed brilliant discussions with my six and eight year olds whilst reading 'Good Night Mister Tom' by Michelle Magorian. The book is about an evacuee who has been abused by his mentally ill mother. We talked about mental health, secrets, war, death and sex. All topics which the book covers in the most sensitive way. Then there was David Almond's 'Skellig'. This novel is about a boy who finds an odd man-like celestial creature in his garage. Again, the delicate discussions of mortality, learning, friendships and parenting are beautifully crafted by Almond and we had some amazing conversations at levels of emotional depth I had rarely seen from my children before. Other books we enjoyed together were 'Tom's Midnight Garden' (Philippa Pearce), The Lion the Witch and the Wardrobe' (C S Lewis) and 'Running Wild' (Michael Morpurgo), and these led into topics as diverse as faith, loyalty, feminism, animal rights, evil, emotions etc. Rather than living in fear of having 'the chat' with the kids about sex and relationships, it was the easiest thing in the world to discuss sensitive and emotional issues by using the stories as a way in. This was one of my favourite aspects of home-schooling.

PSHCE: (PERSONAL, SOCIAL, HEALTH AND CITIZENSHIP EDUCATION)

Besides the issues which arose from all our reading (see previous paragraph), we also hit some social and emotional issues head-on as we explored Europe. For instance, on a rainy Saturday in Prague we found ourselves in the midst of an enormous pro-Life march in Prague. We stood very close to the pro-choice campaigners who were loudly and visibly making their own case. This brought on some quite complex conversations with the children. In Germany, Tim and I visited Dachau concentration camp. It was the first of the Nazi concentration camps opened in Germany- in many ways a prototype for the bigger ones which were still to come. We thought long and hard about whether or not to take the children in and although we decided (rightly, I think) not to, we did discuss it with them in quite a lot of detail and were amazed by the maturity and understanding they exhibited. It was an incredibly moving experience to stand in those gas chambers and I hope that our children will get the opportunity to visit Dachau or Auschwitz when they are old enough to cope with its barbarous history. On a lighter note, so many of the bridges that we crossed in European towns had locks on them- gestures of love from amorous couples over the years who lock their initials onto the bridge and throw the key into the river. This led to some sweet and hilarious contributions and questions about relationships.

MUSIC:

There was a very cool 'Feel Mozart' section in the *House de Nature* in Salzburg. Here, we could do voice experiments and feel the vibrations of different sounds. We enjoyed Flamenco in the South of Spain and Galician folk music in the north. There was the wonderfully haunting Fado music of the Algarve and some very cool French singing and dancing in one memorable French campsite on yet another bank holiday! We did take a ukulele with us, but sadly this was less of a success than I had hoped (it turns out learning an instrument requires more patience than my children had in that particular period of time!) but we did manage to educate them in the wonders of 80s movie theme tunes, 90s rock and some superb guitar music of our youth! Before too long, the TV had been turned off in the back of the van and the kids were all enjoying a good old sing-along to 'Wonderwall', 'Are you Gonna Go My Way' and 'Great Balls of Fire!'

LIFE SKILLS:

Not a school subject, clearly, but worth mentioning all the same because this was perhaps one of the most important kinds of learning that happened on our big adventure. The kids learned to wash up independently!

We had VERY RARELY asked them to wash up at home and never on their own- it always seemed too much of a hassle and a liability. But now, with time to spare, the older two could walk off across the campsite together to the basins and get it all sorted without our help. They became more independent in lots of ways, often venturing off alone to purchase things at the campsite shop or explore a new campsite when we first arrived, then

report back and tell us what they'd found. My daughter loved to report back on the toilets. She would give them a score out of ten based on cleanliness, availability of soap, loo paper and hot water. Any facilities with all three things available sent us into raptures!!

The kids also got involved in the cooking and the shopping, they learned to light fires, they helped to empty the van toilet and source drinking water. They also, critically, learned how to adapt to situations that don't quite go to plan. One day, for example, we had planned to leave our campsite in the Ardeche but found we were completely stuck in the mud. The wheels of the van were simply spinning around flicking wet mud up all over everything and there was no grip to get the beast out of the grassy pitch we had parked in. Rather than stress over it or get a tractor to tow us out, we just decided to stay put for another day or two. We simply ate more pain-aux-chocolates and made a mud kitchen for the younger kids to play in. No stress.

ANOTHER TIME, we had booked a canoeing trip down the Sella river, in The Picos de Europa mountain range, Spain. Our youngest was too small to join in so Tim took the older two off with their wetsuits and picnic lunch in a barrel. They were having a wonderful, peaceful time in their canoe for three, spotting a diverse selection of birds and insects and on the look out for the native bears. However, before too long, they hit a rapid at the wrong angle and the canoe tipped over. Tim was able to stay in the canoe but the two kids fell out. Aged six and eight they were decent swimmers but not terribly experienced in such wild conditions and I think it is fair to say that there was a degree of panic. Our eldest son bravely clung to the side of the canoe while Tim shouted instructions to our daughter (who had been nervous about going anyway). Before too long he was able to lift her out of the water and get the canoe over to the river bank so that our son could also climb back in. Now, if I had known this was happening, I would have been beside myself with worry because I know my daughter can be so easily frightened. I would have been worried that she would never forgive me for persuading her to go. However, I had underestimated her. She not only composed herself, she got back in the canoe, carried on and had so much fun that she even elected to do the final 'optional' stretch of river, extending their time by another couple of hours. When they got back to me they were all so proud of themselves and I have never seen my daughter look so pleased with herself. The capsizing had only added to everyone's sense of adventure and bravery. This adaptability and flexibility to overcome problems is a quality that we all continued to develop as the months went on and I think it is one of the most useful skills we could have instilled in our children. I hope it will stay with them for a very long time.

NOT JUST FOR THE KIDS

So, although many people thought of our trip as one big holiday, in many ways it really wasn't. Because you can't *holiday* for a year. After a while, the call of ice-creams and beaches wears off, and we found ourselves able to take much more time than we ever would on an actual holiday to properly explore and *learn* about the places we were in. With no clock to watch or jobs to do, we had energy to share with our kids. We all found ourselves really thinking and talking about the things we were seeing rather than glossing over them before quickly moving on to the next place. Everyone *wanted* to learn. And Roadschool wasn't just for the children. Tim and I were also enriching and deepening our own understanding of the world in a way we hadn't quite anticipated. Whilst we travelled through Spain, I was driven to read a book about Spanish history-something I would never normally find the time to do-and it was because I wanted to understand the things we were seeing. As we travelled Scandinavia, Tim read all kinds of book about the Vikings because it was all so much more real and visceral. We would occasionally take ourselves off to go on a solo walking tour of a city or to visit a gallery because we *could*. None of it was an effort or a chore and it was one of the most enriching educational experiences of the children's lives and of *our* lives.

Honestly, I could fill this book with the kinds of learning opportunities that Europe handed us on a plate. I began this chapter by saying that although we often justified our year's roadschooling by telling people that I was a teacher, I honestly think that any parent could access and make the most of the learning opportunities that travelling presents. Being a teacher wasn't what enabled me to teach the kids. Just being in these places, with time on our hands, was all we needed. We were enjoying this incredibly rich experience and we all had time to indulge in the details. It was pure magic.

And we didn't have to work very hard at all to extend these amazing opportunities into further learning for the kids on the quieter days either. They wrote stories about friendships forged through the Berlin wall, or Viking children who survived harsh winters and about children trapped on wild islands like the one we visited off the coast of Dubrovnik. Their imaginations were in overdrive. They didn't need learning objectives or assessments or writing frames. They were reading, writing, learning and thinking every single day and I know I sound smug, but what I am trying to say is that education is everywhere and if you're considering taking your children off travelling but frightened that you won't know how to teach them- allay those fears right now; the world will teach them. All you have to do is go and show it to them!

UNSCHOOLING?

It is fair to say that my views on education have changed enormously as a result of this experience. Having spent almost my entire life in educational institutions, I suddenly found myself learning more than ever before by stepping *out* of education. I used to be a firm believer in the fundamental necessity of schools to maintain a functioning society. I no longer feel quite so sure. Before we left, I would have laughed at the idea of homeschooling and I had never heard of the 'unschooling' movement. Unschooling proposes that children learn best when learning is led and directed by their own interests. It questions all conventional forms of schooling, instead advocating learning through playing, seeing, experiencing, curiosity and social interaction. Quite frankly, two years' ago I would have thought the idea preposterous. Now I see it as quite wonderful. More than wonderful, I see it as true and pure. Most people never get the chance to see unschooling in action. Not many parents have the opportunity to see how their kids can be motivated, self-guided learners. It's too much of a risk isn't it, to pull your kids out of school and 'see how they get on'? But for me, as the trip progressed and we ran out of learning books (or motivation to do the learning books), I saw, first hand, how the kids would take themselves off to the beach and set up a pintxos bar. They constructed the shop from bits of driftwood and beach debris. They made a selection of pintxos (inspired by the amazing array of colourful bar foods they had seen on offer in San Sebastian) out of shells filled with seaweed (to them this was spinach), sand (cheese), red string (chilli) and broken shells (tuna). They came up with their own, rather complex, pricing structure and played for hours taking turns to be the shop keeper, customer and waiter. They were self-differentiating according to ability with the elder two doing the times-tables needed for pricing and the younger one counting them out. The menu was written into the sand. My job for the day was done. All I needed to do was get them to the beach (and as we had slept just ten yards away from it, that wasn't much of a challenge). Then they educated themselves.

THE DOWN-SIDES

"Come on though!" I hear you shout. 'Homeschooling must have had some drawbacks?" Sure. It did. There were days when I had to cajole and badger my reluctant kids to get involved in some learning.There were times when all they wanted to do was build Lego models but my inner good-grammar-school-girl-self was riddled with guilt that they should really be learning their times tables. (I tried using Lego to teach them multiplication-they told me not to poison their favourite toy!). There were occasional tears (*mostly* from the kids) because they "didn't get it" and times when I would have given my left arm to have had access to some learning games on the internet but instead, I was stuck trying to convince the three of them that they did really enjoy working from "boring old books". There is also the matter of headspace. It would be a lie to say I didn't sometimes fantasise about what I planned to do with a day to myself once I could drop them off at school again in September. It's important not to underestimate what a bit of time of your own can do for a parent. It's true that homeschooling doesn't allow for very much 'me time'.

Another interesting insight into education came from meeting other travelling families. Those first friends we made, the Brave-Brightons, turned up again on our campsite in San Sebastian and we had the chance to spend almost a week in their company. They had previously been on a global gap year with their kids and had chosen to homeschool in the interim period before heading off around Europe in their camper van. When I asked them about their experiences of homeschooling, I recall Justin's wistful face as he reminisced the ideals he had envisaged before they had embarked upon homeschooling.

"I imagined the kids waking up each day and working through

some Maths puzzles, then doing some writing. Maybe an examination of something under the microscope and then some art in the afternoon." He and Tams shrugged as they admitted that the reality of long-term home-schooling for them had been quite different. "In fact," his wife Tamzin added, "it turns out life doesn't really stop and allow you all this time to sit down with the kids. There's still a baby to feed and get to sleep and a mountain of washing to do and finances to sort. Where's the time?" At the beginning of the trip I was a bit taken aback by what I was hearing. It seemed as though their home-schooling experiment hadn't been quite as halcyon as I'd imagined. But I got to know their kids and, by gosh, were they awesome. Their eldest, at ten years old, was the kindest, most mature and charming girl I had ever met. She had obviously been quite heavily involved in raising her baby brother and she had such a gentle, open manner. She was delightful with my kids. She also read more than any other young person I have known before. She loved books and had the time to really indulge in them. Much as I laughed to see her hauling a sewing machine out of the back of their van (*how* they had room for a *sewing machine* in their campervan was beyond me!), I was amazed to see her get on with sewing little clothes for Sylvanian Families and beautiful decorations that she gave out as gifts. And their son- well he was a dab hand with a knife at five years old. He was sensible and safe and careful and could whittle sticks at whim. He knew how to light a fire and could swim like an absolute fish. Maybe, by UK schooling standards, these kids didn't have everything. The older daughter confessed that her grammar wasn't always perfect and the little boy hadn't yet learned to read. But they were skilled in so many other ways. And so wordly-wise. Besides that, they were awesome people. The kind of kids you could happily spend hours with. I did a lot of thinking about those children and how different they were to the institutionalised young people I knew in the UK. The most striking difference was how free they were. The sense of freedom they felt in their lives shone out from their faces and the same could not have been said about any of the children I'd ever taught in a school.

The Brave-Brighton family, as it turned out, didn't return to England. They found a plot of land in the Portuguese hills. They now grow olives, figs, apricots, oranges, walnuts, and a whole host of other things. Their social media posts (which are few and far between - they clearly are not slaves to the internet) show smiling, bronzed faces. They are in yoga poses or sat peeling fruit or running though trees and that look in their faces- that freedom- shines even brighter than before. It is impossible not to envy them and their decision to choose a different kind of life. I know it can't all be perfect. I know that their new life must also come with its own share of complications and problems, but I believe that their choice to abandon the expectations of normality can be an inspiring lesson to us all.

AN INTERNATIONAL PERSPECTIVE ON EDUCATION

A month or so later, we befriended a Swiss family. They had *four* kids in a caravan and were also on the road for a year. What was really striking was the different challenges they had faced in escaping their national school system. The couple explained to us (in perfect English) that in Switzerland it is illegal to home-school your children. They had to fill in an extraordinary quantity of forms in order to apply for permission to take their kids out of school for a year and had fully expected their application to be denied. They explained that such situations are almost always refused. By a stroke of luck, or perhaps (as they believed) with God's intervention, they were granted permission but there were some very strict conditions and their progress was being monitored by the local education authority. Their experience had been so different to ours and it made me wonder how much any of our governments really know about home-education, or education in general really.

As an aside here, this Swiss family were on their big road trip because they believed that God had given them a mission. They were there to pray with the poor and needy on the streets and to try to establish a new church community. Now, rightly or wrongly, Tim and I would never normally spend very long in conversation with such an evangelist couple. We would smile politely and extricate ourselves from the situation. However, our new life, our new way of looking at the world, meant that we found ourselves feeling much more open minded and tolerant of difference (plus, living in a tiny van, full-time with three kids means that any kind of adult conversation takes on a whole new level of interest!). We opened our minds to their beliefs and choices and we enjoyed a few glasses of wine bonding over all that we had in common.

When we were in Austria, I had an illuminating conversation with a German lady. Her son was seven and, despite, not speaking any English he was enjoying several games of cards and football with our lot. She sat down for a chat with us and after we got through her bemused questioning about Brexit, we also got chatting about schools. She said her son had started school age last year, aged 7, and that he still only attended for the mornings, coming home each afternoon. She couldn't really understand why, in the UK, we send them to school aged 4 and leave them there all day. It was obvious from her tone that she found our system a little barbaric. She asked "when do the children have time to play?" And "when do they relax?" and "How do they develop their physical skills- when do they climb trees and go for bike rides?" I could certainly see her point. And her seven year old son seemed to be doing a pretty good job of beating my kids at Uno and scoring a few goals past them. No-one can claim that the Germans are lagging behind us in terms of ingenuity and progress; in fact quite the opposite is true. We had similar conversations with Swedish, Dutch and Danish families. All pretty confused about how our four year old son would be starting full-time school that September. A friendly Croatian campsite owner told us about how all Croatian children, at every age, only attend school until lunchtime every day. My kids thought this sounded like a brilliant idea! I don't know if it stems from their limited educational funding or if it is a hangover from a time when families needed their children home to help with the family business. But in such a hot country, and as a teacher myself, I can see a lot of sense in doing away with afternoon lessons. Picture a steaming hot classroom, full of children who have eaten lunch then run around in the sunshine for an hour. Believe me, very little learning happens in afternoon lessons, especially when it's hot. Perhaps this schooling model enables families to spend more time together and for learning to be condensed and purposeful.

So, I finished our trip with an entirely new perspective on education. I no longer felt like schools were essential or always helpful. I had begun to feel that the focus, in schools, is sometimes ill advised and misdirected and I was becoming increasingly convinced that 'unschooling' had its merits. I certainly knew that travelling and seeing the world was the best kind of education a child could get and that having the freedom to play, read, be active, think and breathe was a sure-fire way to gain ignite a child's imagination, health and creativity.

* * *

***PS. Post Script: Having fallen in love with home-schooling, Tim and I spent many, many long hours sitting in the van trying to work out a way of long-term living that would enable us to keep educating the children in this way. We came up with one hair-brained scheme after another: first we thought we might live in the van for good, living for six months in Southern Europe (probably in Spain) and then journey back to the UK so that Tim could get some temporary work to fund the six months abroad again (but then our grown-up selves admitted that there was no security in this and if one of us got sick, we'd be in major trouble); so then we thought perhaps we'd buy a big house in rural France (for very little money- you can buy a six bedroom house in Normandy for £75,000!Seriously- Google it-you'll be amazed!) . We figured Tim could commute and I would homeschool the kids in France (but then we thought about how rubbish that would be for Tim who would spend a long time away from us. We would probably both get pretty lonely); The next plan involved me applying for and working in an International school somewhere lovely and warm in Europe. The kids could attend the school and Tim could ...hmmm... we couldn't work out quite what Tim could do! Eventually, after much deliberation we reached the decision that we needed to come back to the UK, for Tim to have some job security, to recoup what he has paid into his pension and, after all, there was a lot that we missed about normal life. We tried not to let the kids know that we were considering an alternative future. As far as they were concerned, we were only ever going away for the year and then returning to our home town. Over the year it became clear that they had mixed feelings about this. The eldest, who I had felt sure would enjoy the trip the most, longed to get back to school. Middle child, who I had been most worried about, said she never wanted to return to school.*

Little one, who had been running feral for a year had turned totally wild and I was terrified he would find school a serious challenge.

Now, having been back for a few months, and put the kids back into school, there isn't a day that goes by when I don't wonder if we did the right thing by coming back. Having seen all the benefits of home education, I now die inside when I see how packed the children's classes are and the over-stretched nature of the resources in school. I hate to hear of them spending a lonely hour in the playground, unable to find anyone to play with, or a bored afternoon doing work that is too easy for them. In a way, I find it difficult to reconcile my new outlook on life with the very staid and traditional way in which schools educate our young people. The transition has also been challenging for the kids. "Of course it has!" people almost laugh in my face, "they got to travel every day for a year, see incredible places and have a whale of a time. Real life isn't like that." I'm not an idiot, I realise that these people are absolutely right. But the thing is, what these people don't seem to realise is that real life CAN be like that. That was our real life for a year and we've met people for whom that is real life all the time. I think that, too often, we accept boredom and unfairness as necessary ingredients of everyday life and I am no longer convinced that this needs to be the case. I don't now feel frightened to err from the status quo. The trip has given me the confidence to stray from the norm without being too terrified of he consequences; home education is not just for hippies!

So, the jury is out on whether or not we plan to keep the kids in school long-term. We've lived through an alternative method of schooling and, sure, it had its challenges, but it also had so many advantages and it is very difficult, having done it once, to witness my children being bored and unhappy in school when I know I could offer them so much more. However, the reality is that home-

schooling the kids would be an enormous sacrifice on my part. I'd have to give up any hopes of returning to a career in the near future and say goodbye to my chances of earning any money. My relationship with my kids could be enriched by all the time we'd send together or, it could be damaged by a lack of distance from one another. Quite simply, we need to give it time and think it over carefully. But, for now, I haven't written anything off.

* * *

RECOMMENDED RESOURCES

If you're considering your own road trip or if you'd like to know more about Road-schooling, home-schooling or any of the other issues in this chapter. Here are some resources I would recommend:

Learning websites:

www.khanacdemy.org This amazing resource is totally free and has millions of videos and games and exercises to help home educated kids. We found it useful for my eldest child (I'd suggest age 10+). It charts their progress, suggests further learning, helps them to understand tricky topics (the Maths section is particularly awesome) and send you an email telling you what they've done that week. Really, really helpful.

scratch.mit.edu One of the benefits of home-ed is that you can find time to focus on things that schools struggle to accommodate. This superb resource teaches kids to code. It is so user friendly that they can operate it totally unguided by Mum or Dad (if, like me, you have no idea how to code) and was a true favourite with my kids.

www.topmarks.co.uk

There are tons of learning games out there on the web but I find this selection really useful and useable. Maths and English games are organised by type and age and there is tons to work with here.

www.duolingo.com

Brilliantly interactive website which encourages you to practise another language every day. We would do this as a family. I think if we'd had more regular internet access this would have become a much bigger part of our days, but the sporadic wifi we encountered meant we didn't learn as much as would have liked.

For times when there is no internet (Hurrah!), we did find some learning books helpful. There are millions on the market but here are some of the best ones we found (I think a 'good' home learning book can vary enormously according to tastes but here are the ones we liked):

Educational books (for 7-11 year olds):

- *Monster Handwriting practice by Letts*
- *Extraordinary English by Letts (and English Basics)*
- *Developing literacy by A and C Black*
- *Rising Stars Mathematics Key Stage 2*
- *Key Stage 2 Mental Arithmetic by Schofield and Sims (and their KS2 Problem Solving)*
- *Spelling for Literacy by Andrew Brodie (and Improving Comprehension)*
- *Carol Vorderman's English Made Easy*
- *Science Homework Helpers by Pearson*

- *Start Writing Adventure Stories by Chrysallis Children's books.*

INSPIRING 'FAMILY TRAVEL' ***and homeschool social media feeds:***

worldtravelfamily

lifeinourvan

caravanningwithkids

ourfamilytraveladventures

Lulalastic and the hippy shake

Happiness is here

Raised Good

Learning Escapes- Cultural Travel with kids

thenomadicfamily.com

a Boundless Life

Learning Escapes- Cultural travel with kids

Books to read with your kids that will open up interesting discussions about life:

'Goodnight Mister Tom'

'Skellig'

'Tom's Midnight Garden'

The 'My Funny Family' series by Chris Higgins

'The Lion, The witch and the wardrobe' by C S Lewis

Any Michael Morpurgo novels

'Rebel Girls'- each page is dedicated to a different female 'rebel' role model who defied her stereotype and made a difference in the world.

The entire 'Harry Potter' series will open up a world of discussions about morals, values, courage, loyalty, authority and friendship.

CHAPTER 4

FAMILY TIME ON OUR BIG ROAD TRIP

"Five of you living in a tiny van? Didn't you want to kill each other?"

When we set out on our pswelovEU tour of Europe, we knew that lines would be significant. We wanted to show our kids as many of the 28 countries which make up the European Union as possible while the lines between them were still open to us UK citizens. For our family, it was an absolute joy to embrace the freedoms of the Shengen agreement. Often, we shouted back to the kids to brace themselves- we were about to enter a new country. They would peer compliantly out of the camper-van windows only to sink back down into their chairs at the anticlimax of finding that were are no gates or fences. Often, there was barely a sign. Sometimes we stopped to try and take a photo for our social media pages- showing the momentous moment that we entered a new country- only to find that there really was *nothing* to photograph!

"But Mum, everything looks JUST the same!" the kids would call from the back. It was true. It did all look the same. Of course it did, because these border lines aren't really there either are they? Powerful white men with rather basic maps sat down a long time ago and decided where to place the borders but the reality is that the landscape is the same on either side of this imaginary line. The people are the same on either side. Europe is one big unified place and the lines have, in many ways, dissolved over time. I'm not saying the separate countries don't exist. Slovenia was quite a different place to Italy. The Slovenians and the Italians still retain their individual national identities. But they sure like to hop cross the border and shop in each others' stores, eat in each others' restaurants, drink from each others' beer fountains and ski on each others' mountains.

LINES ARE a funny thing aren't they? Especially the ones that don't exist. There were moments on our road trip which we have already started to forget as we look back through rose tinted glasses at our wonderful adventure. Moments, more numerous than I'd care to admit, when Tim and I were tearing our hair out and trying our best to keep sane whilst imploring the kids, once again, to please be aware that they were on the verge of crossing the line between silly (which was tolerable) and crazy (which was not). Imagine the scene: it had been a long day: Team Hammond had explored a new town or city, walked for miles, coaxed the kids into doing some schoolwork, squeezed inside the van once the rain arrived to cook three variations on a meal (to accommodate dietary preferences) in a kitchen measuring 70cmx70cm. Then, squashed into a tiny booth table, we ate said meal and washed up in the same space. Just when we began folding the three of them into their pyjamas, eagerly expectant for bedtime, the kids saw a window of opportunity and engaged in poking/taunting each other/crying because their toothpaste was the wrong colour or their legs had turned 'fizzy'. I truly, truly want to be a hippy, zen-like-parent. It's part of the reason I went on this trip. Sometimes I managed it. In other moments, like these, I did not. There were fireworks. And fireworks in a van are never a good idea!

ONCE THE PEACE had been restored, the kids often apologised "sorry Mummy, I know we crossed over into the crazy-place." Yes, they crossed the line. There's no real line there though, is there? Yet, it exists all the same. If you're a parent (or a teacher), you know all about the line. The line rules your life. It makes all the difference between a high-five of a day and a "please can we go home now?" kind of day. But this line is an unpredictable blighter. It moves around depending on a huge number of factors such as sleep deprivation, quantity of sugar (or alcohol) imbibed, amount of space available etc. In the kids' defence, it was (and is) a tricky one for them to negotiate.

PARENTING IS HARD. It is hard when you live in a big house, it is hard when you live in a tiny van. It is hard when you work full time and it is hard when you are with your kids all day, every day. Before we left our lives behind, Tim and I knew that we weren't quite the parents we wanted to be. This self awareness was a big part of the rationale behind going on our big adventure in the first place. We figured the trip would give us all time to step out of our habits and routines, giving us the time to reset our relationships. We were very conscious that we had become tired, snappy, reactive parents. In some way, our busy modern lives seemed to mean that we were giving what felt like all our time to facilitating our kids' social lives but still not really enjoying any quality time together. By taking everyone and everything else out of the picture, we figured we could really get to know each other and bond in a whole new way. Looking back now, I can say with absolute certainty that this was a hugely successful aspect of our journey.

Some people seem to coast through life, cheerfully shepherding their offspring between school, swimming lessons and taekwondo classes with the minimum of fuss and stress. They don't seem phased by having to attend a committee meeting whilst simultaneously preparing dinner for five and overseeing the tradesmen who are taking three days to repair the toilet (when they promised it would be a five minute job). I used to watch these people in awe, sweat dripping from my brow in the sweltering hot swimming pool changing room, as I forced my daughter's foot into her brother's shoe, then hurried home to burnt casserole, blocked drains and an older son who wouldn't talk to me because I was late collecting him from hockey training. I would wonder why I was finding it all so stressful. I am a capable, healthy, professional woman. I had made a choice to have my three lovely children. Why wasn't it as much fun as I had hoped it would be?

I HAVE NOW WORKED out why we were all so stressed. I think it boils down to one thing- TIME. Suddenly, on our trip, we had time. Sure, we still had our moments and got cross with the kids but essentially there was so much more time to be together. Rather than spending the week dashing about all over the place, leaving just the two day weekend in which to bond and connect (most of which was lost to kids' parties/kids' sporting events/social events or, let's face it, getting over our tiredness from the busy week). Now, on the trip, we had all week to take our time and enjoy experiences together. Everything was slower on the road -at one point we even got overtaken by a hearse!- and this gave a whole new meaning to family time. I've mentioned a number of the big cities and the exciting things we did there. Places like Rome, Seville, Salzburg and Dubrovnik hand you interesting activities on a plate and we almost always had a fabulous time exploring the big names. But, like I said, motorhomes don't get you anywhere very fast and so, inevitably, there were a thousand stops along the way in less glamorous towns, villages, campsites, car parks and fields. These were the places when I most noticed how much time we had. And often, I think these were the kids' favourite places. I remember a little campsite in Tuscany that we stayed at in February. We had left the previous stop with high hopes- in the guide book we could see that the Tuscan campsite we were heading to had a pool and a beautiful backdrop. Novices that we are, we failed to take note of the altitude and as we wound higher and higher up the mountain roads the temperature dropped, and dropped and the piles of snow got higher and higher. By the time we arrived (to the bemusement of the little old lady who ran the place) it was clear we were stuck here for a while- there was no getting out again quickly! Unsurprisingly, the campsite was basically shut, she just stayed open in the hope that a few brave or local souls might come to her restaurant. But, no problem, after a jowly kiss each from our patron (who must have been knocking on ninety years old), we shovelled out a parking space and we sat, between snow drifts, wondering what on earth we were going to do. It's fair to say we were feeling a bit stupid and deflated. No matter to the kids though - they found an abandoned, derelict, plastic play house and used the walls of it as sledges. They spent hours sliding down the hillsides. If for no other reason than to keep warm, Tim and I joined them in building a family of snow people and then once we could no longer feel our fingers, we sat in the old lady's lovely warm restaurant, drinking hot chocolate, eating biscotti and playing umpteen games of Uno. Our charming host also put 'Tom and Jerry' on her TV for us. This programme works in every language and we all sat around laughing and playing. I can hardly think of a time when I have been more relaxed. I couldn't do any washing- the pipes were frozen. We couldn't do any route planning- there was no wifi. There was no homework to do, lunch boxes to pack, people to call, toilets to clean or places to go. There were very limited food supplies in the van so it was pasta with peas and parmesan for dinner. Easy! We just sat in a snow drift and connected with our kids. It might not have been what we'd hoped for from from Tuscany, but it was bliss!

WHAT DID WE DO?

I could tell you a million stories about time that we spent just being together. I guess most of them ended or started with a glass of wine/sangria/beer/coffee/hot chocolate in a bar somewhere (especially early on in our journey, in Spain and Portugal where a coffee routinely cost 75 cents and a glass of wine €1.50!) but there were also some lovely moments playing stuck in the mud on beaches, greedily eyeing up goodies in local bakers, swimming in rivers or municipal pools, building dens and playing football, basketball, table tennis or Quidditch. One brilliant free camper-stop in Slovenia came with the use of a local 3G football pitch, another in France was next to a playground complete with table tennis tables and a basketball court. There was a superb beach-side parking area in Denmark (again it was free of charge) that had a series of little beach-side camping huts which the kids found utterly inspiring and a campsite in the Czech Republic which had twenty or so little ride-on cars that kept the kids amused for hours. We found ourselves playing Dobble or chess tournaments with the kids not because we felt guilty or obliged to but because we literally had nothing else to do! We *wanted* to play with them and I think the kids suddenly had two parents they didn't quite recognise. Ones who were calm, joyful and present; not just in a physical sense but a mental one too.

NOW, we are not religious people but we did visit A LOT of churches on our trip. Often in a European town the church will be one of the main tourist draws and when you've got time on your hands you'll take any distraction offered. It's fair to say the kids weren't always terribly interested in the architecture or the art but I could usually entice them in with the promise of lighting a candle. Now this, they loved! Unlike the UK, with its plethora of safe, battery operated tea-lights which switch on when you insert a coin and press a button (boo hiss!), most places on our trip still offered the exciting chance to burn your fingers on a real flames whilst lighting your candle and saying a quiet prayer. What I loved most about this experience, besides watching the focus and concentration on their little faces and the respectful quiet they could take part in when they really had to, was the conversations we would have afterwards about what they had prayed for. Our youngest always prayed for the same thing "to be safe in this family" *sob* but the older two's wishes and hopes were a brilliant reminder to us of what mature, interesting and thoughtful little people they were becoming. They'd say things like "I said I hope people can stop harming the environment," or "I said I hoped my sister would have a nice birthday," or "I said thank you that we have been able to come on this trip." And just like that, all my stresses and worries would fall away.

OF COURSE, it wasn't all about character development, some of our Roadschooling lessons were about educating our kids in fundamentals like 'proper music'! Long journeys in the van meant we could expose them to some of the very best from our musical culture. Just a few months into the trip they could sing along to Nirvana's 'Smells like Teen Spirit', various Oasis hits and Elvis' 'Jailhouse Rock'. Lenny Kravitz' 'Are You Gonna go my Way?' even became my youngest's favourite song- he can do a very good air guitar solo! Rocking out together was such a cool way of bonding as a family and sharing some of the stories of our own youth with our kids. The songs often led on to anecdotes and stories from our younger days and the children seemed to love hearing our silly memories. In fact, it became a major factor in persuading the kids to help with the washing up at campsites- the promise of some cool songs on the iPhone and one of Daddy's 'funny stories'. He regaled them with tales of how ridiculously naughty he was at school and how mean he was to his brothers. The kids absolutely loved hearing about the sticky situations and scrapes he got himself into and it makes me sad to think how little time we get to really talk to our kids in 'normal life' and how few of these stories they had heard before we set out on our big adventure.

ALONG THE SAME lines as their musical education, the kids also got a bit of a classic-film-education on the road. Yes- there was lots of time spent chatting in bars and watching sunsets but there was also a fair amount of time trapped in a van whilst it blew a gale/poured with rain/froze brass monkeys outside.

On evenings such as this we enjoyed a good squish into our tiny seating area and a family film. Away from the delights of Netflix and on-demand TV, we were limited to our selection of old-school classic DVDs like 'Annie' (old and new- loved them both), Karate kid (old and new- loved them both). 'Swallows and Amazons', 'Harry Potter', 'Mr Bean' and 'The Three Amigos'. Revelling in our new hippy-parent-status we also threw caution to the wind a few times and put on films such as 'Topgun' ("Daddy- why did Iceman just call that guy a 'dead kid'? (he hadn't. Iceman had called him something that rhymes with sick-head!), 'Pitch Perfect' (Mummy what does she mean "sticks and stones may break my bones but chains and whips excite me"?) and, most cringingly, 'Love Actually' (we had only remembered the sweet boy playing the drums in the school play and the bum-wiggling prime-minister scenes. We had totally forgotten about the simulated porn film and all the F-words...).

Maybe some of these were not our proudest parenting moments but we were sharing memories and bonding and the kids absolutely LOVED it! One of the highlights of the filmic education (for me) was watching 'The Sound of Music' (because, seriously, when else can you find three hours to watch it?!) and then dancing with the children around the iconic Mirabell gardens and the sights of Salzburg where the scenes were filmed, (even the "I am sixteen you are seventeen" gazebo), pretending to be the Von Trapp Family. Brilliantly, my Mum came to visit us in Salzburg so she got involved in this too- posing for photos as Maria Von Trapp with my kids dancing alongside her. What a brilliant day- three generations of one family revelling in adoration of this classic film. My Mum swinging her arms in the air as we ran through the gates, just as Maria did, is a moment I will never forget and made for the most fabulous photo!

ONE OF THE most amazing things about our year on the road was the way in which the children played. Given the gift of time and space, they amazed us with the imagination and focus they were now exhibiting in their games. You hear a lot of people talk, nowadays, about how kids so rarely have the opportunity to be bored. This trip, as well as providing our kids with some amazing life experiences, also gave them a fair amount of unattended time to fill. Hours in the van, in campsites and in camper-stops, with no video games, no TV and often no internet meant that they unleashed their creativity in a way I hadn't seen before: they invented games together, like a version of Quidditch that involved a ball, some sticks and several cuddly toys; they built a fort on the beach from abandoned driftwood and bamboo (developing a sound structural awareness); they played for hours with Lego, making entire villages and theme parks (and they even made a set of Lego egg cups one day- both creative AND practical!); they played teddy football; they built a 'duck hotel' in the lake; they skipped and cycled in elaborate formations; constructed dens under trees and one day the eldest made a chess set entirely out of Lego just so that he could give us a game. I know that we sometimes accuse the younger generation of being slaves to their screens; I don't agree with the sentiment entirely, I think computers offer a huge number of creative opportunities, however the change we witnessed in our kids on this year of freedom was a real eye opener and made me wonder just how much we repress their imaginations in our busy, overtimetabled world.

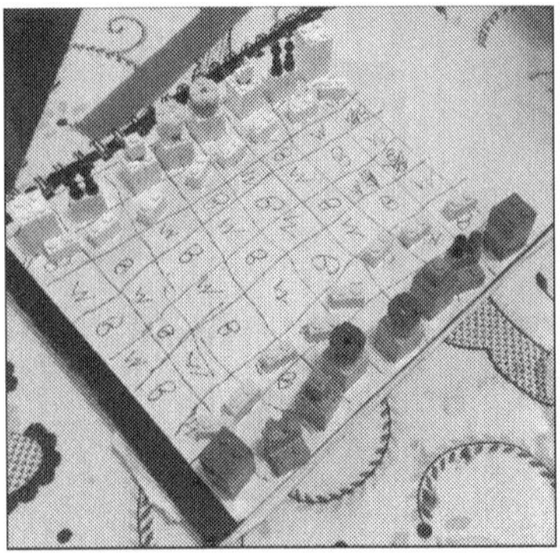

QUALITY TIME WITH THE EXTENDED FAMILY:

Time with the extended family was an interesting element of the trip too. When we set off, there were, as mentioned, some tears from various relatives who were going to miss us and there was degree of pining, by us, whilst we were away for the people who were a big part of our lives and we hadn't seen for a while. Happily, some of those people managed to come out and join us for a few days and it was striking how much we all enjoyed their company. In many ways, I felt that time we spent together was so precious, I wouldn't have traded those few days of quality time for a whole year of the regular haphazard-visits that normally make up the time we spend with friends and family. In Salzburg, Dubrovnik and Pompeii we were delighted to welcome grandparents and lovely friends to share in our adventure for a little while. Rather than staring at each other over coffee and the usual small talk, we found ourselves exploring incredible places together, sharing new cuisines (and plenty of good wines) and really enjoying some big philosophical discussions about what our trip had taught us so far. The kids got the opportunity to venture on cable-car and fast-ferry adventures with their grandparents, and to explore ancient civilisations with their pals. It was superb and we were so grateful for people who had found the time and money to join us. I think there's a lot to be said for valuing quality over quantity here, especially in the age of Skype and social media which helped us all keep in touch, despite the geography. One of the things that most put me off going off like this, on our year abroad was that I felt I would be neglecting these important relationships but in hindsight, if any of you are feeling the same way, I'd urge you to just do it. A year is really nothing in the grand scheme of things. You will find ways of maintaining relationships with all those people who are most important to you and it might even lead to you building and developing those bonds on a whole new level.

CELEBRATIONS:

Thinking of time with the extended family leads me on to to tell you about the big celebration days. I guess Christmas is the time when our relationships with our relatives are perhaps at their most obvious. Christmas without grandparents, nieces, nephews and siblings was a weird one. It was certainly true that Christmas was the time when we we missed everyone most of all. However, I would like to tell you a bit about our festive 2016 because, apart from missing the family, it was the best Christmas we've ever had. It is another brilliant example of how good this road trip was for the five of us.

The run up to Christmas was different. Very Different. Here's the little poem I wrote about it in my blog:

'Twas the week before Christmas

Twas the week before Christmas and no-one was stressed
No puddings were made and no tree had been dressed

No shopping to do or sprouts to forget
No 'work-do' hangover tinged with drunken regret.

It's true that no stockings were hung by the fire;
(there's no room for such things when your house sits
on tyres).
St Nick came already, a few weeks ago
We've no Frosty the Snowman (there's no chance
of snow).

The children aren't nestled all snug in their beds,
They're toasting marshmallows on the camp-fire instead.
No school Christmas fairs or nativity plays,
No Mariah Carey on loop, or jingling sleighs.

But, I have a jolly man (with a beard) who is full of
good cheer
and a bunch of good kids who seem happier this year.
There won't be huge piles of presents, or twinkling lights,
But still a good Christmas, and the most silent of nights.

There was a just a week to go until Christmas, (we were still in Spain) and the local town council had only just put the decorations up in the main square. Can you imagine such tardiness here in the UK? I think our local authority starts stringing the lights up immediately after Halloween! In Spain they hadn't been playing Christmas songs on repeat in the shops since November and was no-one rushing around the supermarkets like there was an urgent need to stock up for an impending nuclear-holocaust (except that is, for the one day we popped over to the British island of Gibraltar to get some mince pies-*there* it was total carnage-it felt just like home)!

But, like Spain itself, I too was apparently unruffled. Normally by mid-December I have baked dozens of delicious Christmas treats, wrapped thousands of presents and written millions of heart-felt messages in Christmas cards to the teachers, bin men, distant relatives, long-lost friends and neighbours-whose-names-I-don't-know (Dear all at Number 18...). Living in the van meant that baking had been very limited, decorations were sparse and presents were necessarily few and tiny. Obviously, we hadn't attended any of the typical Christmas functions which usually fill December's calendar page; the school Christmas fair, the nativity play, the work-do, the drinks with friends, the family gatherings, the grotto visits etc etc. I was feeling strangely calm and unaffected by it all.

IN MANY WAYS this was nice. In fact, truth be told, I had been looking forward to a different kind of Christmas. Despite outwardly acting like the embodiment of the Christmas spirit, I, like many of us, harbour deep misgivings about the excess and commercialism of a British Christmas. I think the build up is criminally long and I hate the way kids live under the fear of not being on Santa's good list for weeks and weeks. For me, the need to project some kind of picture-perfect Pinterest-style image of my family Christmas can feel a little overwhelming. In previous years I have been secretly drowning in over-tired, stressed out and ungrateful kids who haven't appreciated me dragging them around the cold, over-priced Christmas attraction, but Facebook only ever saw the one photo I got of them smiling (because I bribed them with the promise that we could go home and watch TV soon).

THEN THERE ARE THE PRESENTS. Oh man. Every year I feel a bit sick at the grotesque number of presents my children open. They come home from school at the end of term with the little pack of stickers or colouring book from their teacher and I see their absolute delight in it. Perversely, I envy the teacher for getting in with that first gift, the one they can really enjoy. They colour it in, use up the stickers and delight in its inexpensive brilliance. But once Christmas really gets going, how much time and play are spent on the other gifts? The stocking fillers are enjoyed for an hour or two but then the relatives arrive, each with another thoughtfully-chosen, brilliant and expensive gift (or three) but with each unwrapping I can see my kids becoming more and more overwhelmed. My husband and I urge the kids to pay attention and be grateful but all the poor kids really want to do is play with the thing they opened an hour ago. We chastise them and remind them that there's no time for that- we need to open the next one and the next one. I sound ungrateful, I know, but I don't blame the lovely relatives. I can't judge them for wanting to see the joy on my kids' faces as they open the gift their hard-earned-money has bought. Only it doesn't usually work out that way. I end up desperately expressing the gratitude my kids are too exhausted to muster. Anyway, you get the picture. You probably live it too. Maybe other people manage it better than we do? But we have three kids at our tree and we both come from quite large extended families; although this is an absolute blessing it also creates a bit of a gift avalanche!

SO, 2016 was set to be different. A van Christmas, I hoped, would help us avoid this commercialist quicksand. Our kids were set to only receive the few little bits Santa would bring and a gift from each of their siblings. But could I relax and enjoy it? No. The guilt set it. You know the Christmas-movie-magic-guilt. As the big day got closer I felt crushed by anxiety that I might be denying my children the "most wonderful time of the year", that maybe I was stealing a bit of their childhood and they would never forgive me. I also felt under pressure to make sure the day was still as special as we could make it- the need for it to be perfect unfortunately didn't get left behind at the white cliffs of Dover. It followed me on my road-trip. And actually, joyful as it is, travelling is hard enough without having to try and make a day magical.

So how did it go? Here's a breakdown:

The day: Christmas day was awesome. The small people opened their (very small) stockings with glee. They all squished into the bed in the middle of the van and we were able to watch them from the warmth and comfort of our own bed. The gifts kept them so happy that we didn't get up until about 10am! With no entertaining to do or place to get to, we could take the day at a MUCH slower pace than usual and this was bliss. I actually HELPED them to make their Lego. I actually SAT and read the new books. We all PLAYED the new game. I never usually find the time for this stuff on Christmas Day and we all really enjoyed this gift of *time* together.

The dinner: Cooking Christmas dinner in the world's tiniest oven/kitchen felt like one of those stupid challenges in the Masterchef final. I cannot deny that this was HARD. Number One Son insisted that it just wouldn't be Christmas without stuffing AND pigs in blankets. As I could only put one teensy tray in the oven at any one time, serving a plate of hot food to everyone made me feel as though Greg Wallace should be presenting me with a medal. However, serving Christmas dinner always feels like that to me and this year, as I hadn't already eaten three different Christmas dinners in the run up, and in fact hadn't eaten a roast dinner for several months, I did really enjoy the food.

Then, the strangest thing happened. I realised I had forgotten to buy (or make) anything for dessert. Anyone who has been fed by me would struggle to believe this-but it's true. I had been so worried about the dinner that I totally forgot about pudding. Imagine how much this would have stressed me out at home. But, this year, no bother- we walked down to the beach, in the sunshine, and bought ice-creams at the beach cafe which we ate whilst watching the waves. Perfection.

The presents: Space in the tiny van was at a major premium. There was simply no room for any more stuff. This was probably the only reason I stuck to my guns and kept the presents to a minimum; I got a serious attack of the fear in the run up to Christmas that the children would never forgive us for depriving them like this. Just the day before Christmas I caved and bought them each a a Lego set to add to the football shirts we had bought them. But do you know what? They didn't care a jot. I know no-one wants to hear from a smug-hippy-"oh-my-children-are-so-not-materialistic"-moron. Let's be clear here, it wasn't exactly the Waltons or Tiny Tim's last Christmas. My kids received about nine small things each from Santa, two things from us and a gift from each other. Let's face it, they are still amongst the luckiest children on the planet. But for us this was a real change and a serious reduction in gifts. As it turned out they were the happiest and most grateful I have ever seen them. Truly. In fact, the joy they got from buying each other (and us) a gift and giving these gifts out was an absolute joy to witness. I plan to work hard to somehow keep the gifts to a minimum now that we are back in the real world again because truly, less IS more.

The people:

This one was the most difficult. There was certainly a sense that this was a rather *flat* Christmas. I did feel a bit sad not to have attended any festive parties. My kidneys were grateful not to have been out drinking with almost everyone I know *because come on-it's Christmas* but my heart was heavy to have missed Mr and Mrs Fun's festive shin-dig and New Year with our best friends and my Christmas night out with the girls etc. Motor-homing is pretty sociable for all those retired people who surrounded us on campsites but they seemed less keen to invite our bunch of noisy kids into their boozing circles! Grown up chat was top of my Christmas list for 2017!

And family? Well, there's no denying it, the worst part of our alternative Christmas was not spending time in the company of our lovely relatives. I felt lucky that we both have plenty of siblings which meant that the grandparents weren't left alone on Christmas Day but I did feel sad to not give them all a big Christmas hug and make fun of them when they fell asleep on the sofa whilst we played silly Christmas games around them. It didn't ruin Christmas but it certainly did play on my mind that there was something missing.

All in all, this was one of my favourite ever Christmases. It wasn't perfect, but then, is it *ever*? It was certainly MUCH less stressful and frenetic than our normal festive season. Christmas dinner in the tent and Christmas day on the beach will be something we will all remember forever. The Spanish traditionally eat twelve grapes, one on each chime of the clock, as midnight falls on New Year's Eve. They do this to bring good luck in the new year. As we did exactly this, Tim and I realised how lucky we already were. We didn't really need the universe to bring us any more good fortune. We had hoped that this trip would help us to re-evaluate what was important to us. In that regard, and many others, Christmas in the van had been a huge success.

PS.Postscript: As I sit writing this, I have just lived through our first UK Christmas since the end of our trip. Once again I have packed away the tree only to turn around to face the piles of newly acquired 'stuff' that I now need to find a home for in our house. Each child has a large pile of exciting new things but these piles can't stay taking up the living room floor forever! Where will it all fit? And the thing that is most striking is that the three children are not playing with their expensive new toys; they are currently playing with the box that the new hoover just arrived in. They have been involved in this game for quite some time. One of them is a robot and the others are- I think- trying to recycle it! I sigh as I remember the modest Christmas we had last year in the camper van and how much that taught me about what

children really want. Despite my best efforts, and pleas to friends and family not to go over the top, the kids still received too much this year. We ate too much, we wasted too much, we threw away FAR too much. It is harder than I thought to bring all the lessons that we learned on our adventure home with us. We got sucked back into the plasticated, over-dressed, over-priced UK Christmas. And all my children really want is this cardboard box. Somehow we seem to have got it all wrong...

OTHER CELEBRATIONS on our big gap year were equally humble and low-key and all the better for it. One of the kids' birthdays was celebrated with some candles in an ice-cream and a trip to the local pizzeria. The youngest one spent the day learning to ride his new bike then playing some silly party games (using potatoes and balloons) with his brother and sister. The eldest had his birthday in February and we were lucky enough to have visitors with us at that point so we held the 'Beach Olympics'- egg and spoon races, three-legged races, throwing the discus (using big stones) and wheelbarrow races. We finished the day with a bonfire on the beach. I was slightly traumatised to discover that 'cake' as we know it, is simply not a 'thing' in Italy (at least not anywhere near Pompeii), so he had a birthday tiramisu instead and he couldn't have cared less. As I tucked him into his snug little bunk bed at the back of the van he said it had been "the best birthday ever," and he genuinely meant it. All that money we spend on presents and expensive parties and coordinated party bags/tableware/decorations- I'm not sure kids care about that stuff at all. It's not just the kids either. On my own birthday we woke up in what was essentially a German-hippy-commune, on the Spanish coast. A place we had stumbled across completely by accident. Basically, just a very isolated patch of rubble and derelict buildings next to the sea that hundreds of (mostly) German people have kind of squatted on and made their own. Most people live there for months at a time, sharing dinners and campfires and the odd bit of wacky-backy. Not the most salubrious birthday venue! There were no showers, no toilets, no running water, but I woke up to the most beautiful sunrise shining off the water, with happy kids and no job to go to and I felt like the luckiest woman in the world. (Don't let me fool you too much though. Later than day we drove to an all-singing, all-dancing campsite with its own spa; so I was able to get clean again in a pool full of lemons! It wasn't all roughing it. But I did enjoy the yin and the yang!).

EAVESDROPPING

Having so much time together and nowhere else to go also meant that the kids heard a lot of conversations that year that they might not ordinarily have been party to. For instance, I'll never forget waking up, glancing at my phone and seeing that Donald Trump had been declared the next president of the USA. It was impossible to keep my frustration and incredulity inside and I vented at length about what a bad outcome this was going to be for mankind. Now, having heard all this, the kids asked what was going on and we had time to explain to them how politics works and why we had been so hopeful when Barack Obama was in office and why we were worried now. There was a similar conversation when the Tories called their disastrous election in the UK, not winning enough seats for an overall majority. When they decided to govern in partnership with the DUP in order to avoid a hung parliament, we got talking to the kids about feminism, homophobia and gay marriage. And we were amazed at how mature and insightful they could be about some challenging issues. At home, I think I might have been in a hurry (as usual) and glossed over these issues which mean so much to me, but having the time to talk them through with our kids like this showed me how much more our kids are capable of dealing with if we only give them a chance.

PS. Postscript: In fact, all this political chat may have transformed our kids into burgeoning activists. At the outset of the trip, our daughter would NEVER, EVER break a rule or put a foot out of line. She was one of those kids who would rather die than lie about their age to get to ride the bigger slide at the water park. Or who would read the notice at the play area that said it was for 2-6 year olds and then the day after her seventh birthday never play in there again (despite the hundreds of other bigs kids gleefully ignoring the rules). It actually became so restrictive at times that we would beg her to break just one little rule. Just sometimes. Plllleeease! Delightfully though, on the trip, we did begin to see a change in her. Partly inspired by the brilliant 'Matilda' soundtrack which we played on repeat ad infinitum (Matilda sings that "sometimes you have to be a little bit naughty") and partly a response to her watching us break a few rules (but only the silly ones like 'tight swimming shorts MUST be worn') and live to tell the tale, she began to get a bit braver. By the end of the trip we had her smiling and saying scornfully "who makes the rules?" as she recklessly went head first down the water slide and kicked a football around the basketball court. Now she has returned to school, and she came home the other day and told me that she'd been called up in assembly for an 'attendance award' due to her 100% attendance at school last term. I don't think I've ever been more proud of her than when she smiled and reported that, in protest, she didn't go and get her reward. She said "because Mummy, I don't think children should be rewarded for something that they often have no control over. People can't help being sick, or having to go to hospital appoint-

ments, so I don't think it's right that people get left out of winning prizes when they can't help it." A very proud parenting moment!

Other conversations the kids overheard that they wouldn't normally were the squabbles and differences of opinion between the two of us. In our home lives we, like many other people I'm guessing, usually quietly simper over something that has annoyed us then raise it with the other partner once we're out of the earshot of the kids. It usually means that we nurse a grievance all day before detonating it into a huge row after bedtime. This is clearly not the healthiest way to maintain a relationship and I think living in such confined conditions on the trip made it impossible. Any rows we had were played out in front of the children and rather than this being a negative, I now recognise it as a very positive thing. The best thing of all was that they also got to witness our reconciliation and peacemaking process. It occurs to me that they so rarely got to see this part before. I'm forever telling them to "make friends again" or "say sorry" but when did they ever see us model it to them? We didn't normally. We used to hide away from their ears and eyes, in the vain hope that they would't know we were fighting. But what message does this send? Kids need to know that it is OK to fight with your best friends and your family. That fights don't mean you aren't a good team. That fights are a part and parcel of being in a relationships and actually, learning to resolve disputes is a massive part of growing into a well-rounded person. I think the necessity of having to solve our issues largely in the presence of the children whilst on our trip helped us all to resolve conflict in a more civilised and open manner.

THE CULTURE OF FAMILY:

Thinking about family life on our trip also reminds me of one significant observation we made in the Southern parts of Europe. Here, 'family' seemed to be a very different notion than it is in the UK. It was common to see extended families spending time together. Grandparents, young kids and, noticeably, teenagers would be out in restaurants, cafes or town squares all together, enjoying food, drinks or leisure time. And bars and restaurants are not reserved for childless adults in Spain, Portugal and Italy. In fact it is totally normal to take your children out for an evening drink. We were welcomed into venues like this all over these warmer climes, often the children would be petted and kissed and almost always given sweets or other little treats by the barman or waiter. After a few months in Spain, Portugal and Italy, as we headed up towards Austria, the children were horrified not to be given a little dish of candy when we ordered coffees. Not that in other European countries the children weren't made to feel welcome, it was just that in the South they were welcomed with wide open arms. I recall being in a Metro station in Barcelona when a young male, maybe late teens or early twenties, smiled and reached out to ruffle my little boy's hair as he passed him on the escalator. My very English instinct was to tense-up in fear and concern at a stranger touching my child, especially a young man, but I looked around and saw that this is just the way in Spain. Children are celebrated by everyone. And also, unlike the UK, there doesn't come a point at which teenagers are sent off to live in their own little world until they re-emerge again as adults. I am a senior school teacher and I see, all the time, the way in which we alienate and remove ourselves from our young people's lives (and I think we do a similar thing to elderly people). We act almost as if teenagers are another species. I saw an alternative in Southern Europe and it looked a much nicer way to live.

IN SPAIN, you see children out playing in the playgrounds- that sit so cleverly alongside the bars- late into the night and no-one is judged or phased by it. Teenagers hang out in the same spaces as everyone else and no-one runs scared of them like we do in the UK. I remember having a few hours to kill with our youngest one day in a lovely little town in Northern Spain. I took him on what, in the UK, would be known as a 'bar crawl'. We visited four or five little wine bars and in each one he could sit with me at the counter, eat the pintxos, enjoy a chocolate milk or a juice and chat to the waiters who patted his head, squeezed his cheeks and fed him free sweets and biscuits. Without fail. They just seemed utterly delighted to have a little boy come and join them in their bar. There is no part of me that can imagine doing anything like this in the UK. I don't know if it's the climate (those lovely long ,warm evening certainly help) or the economy or just the culture but public spaces in Southern Europe seem open to everyone, all day long and it makes for such a charming and welcoming environment.

WHILST WE WERE in Spain we met up with an old school friend of mine. I hadn't seen her since we were 18 but the wonders of Facebook had helped us to stay in touch and we agreed to meet in Xabia, her home town. Half Spanish herself, Ana had lived most of her life in the UK, married an Englishman and had two sons here but had longed to move to Spain. A year before our big trip Ana and her husband had taken the plunge and relocated their lives to this coastal town in Alicante. We met them in one of the bars on the sea front- right next to the superb beach playgrounds- and got to listen, with more than a little envy, to how much their life had changed since emigrating. Both Ana and Ian had been stunned by how different Spanish family life was. They confirmed the things that we had observed- children were much more welcome in Spain and given more freedom. The climate meant that most weekend days were spent at the beach or by the pool and unlike the UK where Ana recalled being stuck in 'kids' zones' like the soft play or the park, or Saturday morning screenings of awful kids' films, here weekends were spent in communal zones. The beach and the bars are full of the elderly, parents, teens and young kids. People aren't segregated off into their own specific zones like we are in our own little pocket of Europe. They told us how, in Spain, school was much less of a focus for everyone. There is no competitive parenting and life is much more about the hours after school which are spent with your family, and the late nights so common to Spanish kids mean that everyone gets so much more relaxed time together. I listened to her and remembered my own frantic after-school hours which were spent rushing from one activity to the next, hectic teas and then an early bedtime. Her way did sound better. It was easy to see why they loved their life in Spain and I confess that we were more than a little tempted to join them. We may have looked in *a few* estate agents' windows that evening!

FRIENDSHIPS:

For all of us, the notion of friendship changed whilst we were on our trip. I desperately missed my friends whilst others in the van, being less sociable souls, were more than happy to maintain contact over the internet and rather enjoyed the insular family unit. However, when the opportunity arose to make a new friend, nomadic life meant we had to grab it with both hands and move fast! We never really stayed in one place for too long- I think three weeks was our longest time staying still and that was only because, before we left the UK, I'd got the colly-wobbles about how well we'd endure winter in the van. In fear, I booked us into an insanely cheap Air BnB apartment on the Algarve, for three weeks in late November/early December. I figured we might need a bit of respite from the van by that point and a bath/kitchen/bit of living space. In fact, when we moved in, we all rather hated being stuck in one place and we were absolutely itching to get back on the road again after about a week. Anyway, for the majority of the trip, an extended stay in one place would mean a week at the most and so that didn't give anyone very long to forge gentle friendships over time. If we spotted someone who looked like a kindred spirit, we had to put our social anxieties to one side and jump in. It was brilliant to see the kids eye up a new campsite, scoping it out for any other children (most times there were none). As the months wore on they became bolder and better at smiling, trying out a greeting in the local language and then kicking a friendly ball in the direction of the targeted child, or offering to share the diggers and lego bricks. We too had to act in ways that were very un-British. For instance, we were chilling out in a lovely park in central Ljubljana when we overheard a couple nearby talking English to their young daughters. WHOOP WHOOOP, the klaxons sounded in my head- here are some people I can talk to who don't sleep within five feet of me every night! I got chatting instantly to the lady-she was utterly delightful. She was an American living in Slovenia while her husband played Pro Ice-hockey there, seeing out the end of his pretty successful career. Gradually, the men-folk were drawn into the conversation and we whiled away a good hour hearing from them about Slovenian life and getting tips from them about cool things to do with the kids while we were in Ljubljana. They were really interested in the idea of our trip and so we had plenty to chat about whilst the kids ran off some steam. This is not such an unusual happening, I hear you think to yourself- I talk to strangers in the park all the time. Well, OK, so do I, but ordinarily I wouldn't swap telephone numbers with that stranger and agree to meet them again tomorrow at the soft play. But on this occasion, that's exactly what I did because English conversation was hard to come by! And then after the soft play meeting, (at which our children- who don't always find it easy to make new friends- had found a new BFF in Jenna's lovely daughter) when she invited us back to her apartment for dinner, we found ourselves accepting. And do you know what? We had such a lovely evening. The kids played and then watched a film. We all chatted and drank wine. Jenna even, bless her heart, insisted on giving our eldest son a haircut right there in her living room. I just couldn't get over the kindness that she showed us, having met us just twenty four hours beforehand. It was such a good lesson for us. Going with the flow, saying yes to things, and being open to new experiences and people can be a brilliantly enriching experience.

A CHANGED CHILD:

Everyone in our family changed on this trip. The children became more independent, relaxed and just happier in general. But nowhere was the change more noticeable than in our daughter. This is quite a personal thing to report on and I've thought a lot about whether or not to include the details, for fear of infringing her privacy. But I've decided to talk about it briefly in case we can offer some hope and advice to any parents or carers who might be dealing with a similar situation:

Having a daughter, between two sons, often means that people ask me to report on any differences I observe between raising the different sexes. It's a difficult question: I only have my own little girl's personality to think about but largely, I would answer that raising her has been quite different from bringing up the boys. Our daughter is a wonderful child: she is creative, loving, thoughtful and smart. She adores her brothers and is fiercely loyal to all of us. She is not, however, the sort of child you might label 'easy-going'. For her, life is one long battle with the anxiety she feels around anything and everything. She finds friendships a big challenge and can take time to adapt and adjust to new situations. When I had returned to work, full-time, when she was just starting school, it was an extremely difficult time for her and I felt I had done her a massive disservice. Before we left for our trip, it was her that we worried about the most. Tim and I had no doubt that the boys would enjoy a big adventure but we worried that our daughter might not cope so easily.

As with so many situations, we had wildly underestimated her. Far from being perturbed by the perpetual change and flux of nomadic life she seemed to come out of herself in a way we had never seen before. In the past, she had always been nervous, timid and very unwilling to try new activities. As the time in the camper van wore on though, we began to see a brand new girl who embraced new experiences and showed the kind of courage and determination of which we had not known she was capable. Having previously suffered from night terrors and broken sleep she was now sleeping soundly and happily, not waking until eight or nine the next morning. In the past, we'd had concerns about her apparent lack of empathy but she was delighting us as each day passed with the kindness and compassion she was now showing to her brothers and those around her. She seemed to revel in the safety of being with us all day every day and we began to think that we had 'fixed' her. That sounds a rather unpleasant word- she wasn't broken before, but she could be quite difficult to deal with at times. Her unhappiness and anxiety had often manifested itself in some challenging behaviours and she was now certainly a happier, healthier child.

When we met up with the grandparents, several months into the trip, they couldn't believe the change in her. She was conversing with them openly, cheerfully, confidently. Before, we'd always had to cajole her a little into any talk at all within a group situation. Yet now she had so much to tell them about our adventures and all the things she felt proud of. It was wonderful to witness. Another time I remember she raced her younger brother across the campsite and she smiled as he celebrated his win. She turned to me quietly and confessed:

"Mummy, I let Tiny win and I told him he was a brilliant runner. I learned that if I give him praise it makes him feel really good. And it makes me feel good too." This from a child who had rarely shown any ability to empathise with others before we left. She was growing and maturing in ways that we hadn't anticipated. If anything made me most glad about the choices we had made to go on this big adventure, it was witnessing this transformation in my daughter. I would just add that if you are wondering how your own child might react to such a trip, maybe you could find courage and take heart from our experiences. It honestly did so much good for our relationships with our children, but especially her. We really connected with them all on a whole new level and I can't tell you how much I value that that time we shared.

P.S POSTSCRIPT: *We have been home for several months now and I am depressed to report that our daughter has reverted to her old self. Returning to school has been a huge challenge for her. She is withdrawn and anxious all the time. She struggles with friendships and she desperately misses the trip. It is very difficult to send a child to school who is so unhappy there and we are giving very serious thought to withdrawing her from the system and home-schooling her.*

For all our best intentions, I think we, too, have slipped back into old habits. I think the children miss those calm, carefree parents who had so much time to give. Once again, they have got parents who are stressed out slaves to the systems of modern life. I don't think it has all been for the worse though. There are certainly some elements of the trip which have stayed with us. Those connections we built with our kids are still strong and I think we are all much more open and honest with one another. I certainly find I am able to put things in perspective a little more and that I am able to say "no" to far more of the external things that don't offer enrichment and happiness to our lives. I am also trying to say "yes" to more of the things that do. I hope I am a little more laid back and less reactive. But one thing is for sure- we spend A LOT of time talking about when we can go off on our next adventure and we ALL long to be back on the road.

THE BEST BITS:

As the end of the trip drew ever closer, I began to feel terribly sad and anxious, wondering whether we were doing the right thing by returning to the UK. As a way to try and be mindful of all the wonderful things we had achieved, I sat down with my notepad one afternoon and asked myself if I could make a list of the year's highlights. As I began writing, I was reminded of just how many fabulous adventures we'd had and one memory would lead me into the next as I recalled the incredible moments of joy and wonder we'd experienced on our big tour. I had intended to come up with a list of ten or twenty things but I found myself scribbling down more and more. It made me feel so wonderful to think back on all those happy memories. Well aware that the kids were also feeling a bit glum I asked them, that evening, over dinner, to help me with my list of the 'best bits'. Well, what a happy dinner time that was. We sat out, under the stars, for hours as they added more and more memories to my collection. What was most staggering and, perhaps, rewarding about this exercise was that the things they listed were the little experiences like: den building in the park in Amsterdam; making new friends; sitting outside in the mountains with Daddy and reading Harry Potter for hours; making a mermaid out of rocks and seaweed on the beach; getting brave enough to do bombs in the swimming pool; Daddy telling us stories of how naughty he was at school whilst we did the washing up; eating biscotti and hot chocolate in the cafe at the snowy campsite. And do you know what? This conversation was taking place at the end of trip when we had recently visited both Disneyland Paris and the Danish Legoland. Yet these big, expensive experiences, which people save for years to be able to afford-because we buy into the hype about the kind of 'magical' days we should be providing for our children- these experiences didn't feature AT ALL in the things that the kids mentioned (until we brought them up and got a cursory "oh yeah- that was really good too!"). Tim and I learned a really important and life-affirming parenting lesson that evening about the kinds of things our kids really want from us. They want quiet, honest time with us. They want to spend time playing and getting to know us. And they want space to have fun and be children at their own pace. I feel so blessed that we were able to give them a year of that.

GREAT GAMES TO PLAY WITH YOUR KIDS/WAYS TO KILL TIME WHEN YOU'RE TRAPPED IN A TINY VAN IN THE RAIN:

- **Dobble** Tiny game in a tin. If you don't have it, and you have kids, BUY IT NOW! It is awesome. There are five different ways to play and even three year olds can join in and beat adults. Genius! Great to play in restaurants and bars.
- **Uno** Classic card game. Quick to play and fun for all ages. Can be played with people with whom you don't share a common language. Another game which allows even very young children to join in and it even helps them to learn their numbers and colours! Great to play in restaurants and bars.
- **Bananagrams** Again, a super game for the whole family. Comes in a very neat little fabric pouch so is easily transportable. An adult can play a child and they can enjoy a game which challenges them both whilst still being perfectly possible for the child to win. SO much fun. We spent HOURS playing this. And it make for competitive evening fun between adults too. Wildly infuriating! Quick to play too. Great to play in restaurants and bars.
- **The drawing game** Like consequences- you draw a head each, then fold the paper over and swap. Then you draw a body, then fold over and swap. Then you draw legs and feet. Reveal your monstrous creature and give him/her a name.
- **Flags of the World** by 'Tactic Games': My children are so much better at this than I am. It's embarrassing. However, a tip around 19 countries in

Europe has improved my flag knowledge and Geography significantly! A lovely compact and educational little game.

- **Top Trumps** All and every version. Kills hours and hours (you can find some good educational ones too- I picked up a pack called *Clash of the Titians* in an Art gallery in Malaga and we all got to learn about Renoir/Heironymous Bosch/Frida Kahlo etc as we sat around waiting for our dinner! Genius!).
- Not one for a rainy day but a great way to pass the time and bond together was our **slack-line**. Simply find two firm supports (trees usually but we also made good use of posts on a beach or electricity boxes on campsites!), string it between them, get it taut with the crank then practise your slack line skills. Great for core strength and mindfulness. Fits neatly into a tiny bag.

CHAPTER 5

MARITAL HARMONY IN THE VAN

"I could never spend that much time with my partner. I'd kill him/her."

In our old life, once my husband got home from work, I would try to explain to him why I had shouted so loudly at my daughter that morning when she had a tantrum about my ludicrous suggestion that she wear "any pair of clean socks in her drawer," rather than her favourite ones which were still muddy from yesterday's puddles. My skin would prickle with anger as I realised that his eyes had glazed over. When he began to launch into his own tales of woe about the evils of commuting, I felt my own eyes glaze with ill-repressed envy. It was all I could do to stop myself from ranting about how jealous I was of his commute. How nice, I thought it sounded, to have ninety minutes of peace and quiet in which to read the newspaper or watch tv on his phone. It was becoming quite a major problem for us. He didn't understand my world; he thought I spent all day drinking coffee with my friends and swanning around the shops. I didn't understand his world; I had no idea what kind of pressure he felt, having to financially support the entire family.

It was a little unreasonable of me to ask him to be sympathetic about the levels of stress I felt getting my daughter to put socks on when he was dealing with critical incidents involving violent criminals. But *I* longed to be treated like an intelligent professional, capable of handling serious situations. I couldn't remember the last time I had used my brain or taken a coffee break which didn't involve picking broken, half-chewed biscuit up from the floor and I barely ever got to see the world outside of our little town. My husband and I loved each other very much. The memory of our shared interests and long history kept us (mostly) from indulging too much in our frustrations because we knew they were unreasonable, but we were still in a bit of a stalemate.

SO, we were grumpy parents and a frustrated couple. But suddenly we had a dream, a dream that offered a way out of these stresses for a year. All of a sudden there was that proverbial light in our little tunnel and we ran towards it with gusto. Honestly, I think this trip may have saved our marriage.

AS A COUPLE WHO, in our normal lives, would often find only a few hours a week to spend together, we suddenly had twenty-four hours a day in each others' company. So what did we do with all this time? I think this is an aspect of our adventure that some people find impossible to imagine. A lot of people I have spoken to say "I just couldn't spend that much time with my partner." What's probably the strangest thing to admit is that we really didn't find it difficult to get used to.

THE LUXURY OF SHARED TIME:

Rather than having to spend our time catching the other up on what the kids were going through/achieving or running through next week's schedule of commitments, we now found ourselves needing a little external stimulation for conversation topics. The average length of time on the road for us was three hours a day (we didn't drive every day, we'd often stay a few days in any one place, but when we did drive, three hours was generally the maximum tolerated length of time before mayhem set in). So, on a driving day the kids would settle down and watch a film in the back of the van and Tim and I were left, in the driving seats with hours to fill as we watch the world pass by our window. We got into listening to podcasts. This was never something we had done together before but I really recommend it for getting you talking about some weird and wonderful issues. Sometimes we'd go for something fairly innocuous like 'Desert Island Discs', which would soon see us reminiscing along similar lines to the Radio Four guests. Other times we'd try something high-brow like a 'Ted Talk' or 'Freakonomics'-podcasts which opened up our minds to issues we'd never given much thought to before-like robots taking over all the jobs, sources of global inequality or the 'War on Sugar'. It was so nice to be able to get our teeth into an interesting and engaging topic. I felt the kind of rush I'd had at university as my mind opened up to a bigger world. The same thing happened when we began listening to a brilliant series of podcasts called 'History on Fire' by Danielle Bollelli. This incredibly interesting, erudite and charismatic guy (with a thick Italian accent that you soon get used to) talked us through a diverse set of strange and wonderful histories such as Franklin D. Roosevelt, the Lakota people, Caravaggio and Spartacus (the latter two we listened to in Italy for a chilling sense of authenticity) and the Ice Man (Europe's oldest human mummy). To engage in this way with learning, together, was a really special experience. And essentially it just came from a few clever podcasters putting their knowledge out there into the world and, crucially, us having the time to access it. When, in our normal lives, would we ever find time to do this? Honestly-never. We've been back for six months as I write this and we haven't listened to a single podcast together again.

AND IT WASN'T JUST the driving time. We also found ourselves reading a great deal and we began talking about our reading and sharing books. For instance, we both read an incredible book called 'Sapiens'(by Professor Yuval Noah Harari) about the history of the human race and his theory that political and economic systems function as universal religions. The book blew my mind and I never would have had the patience or determination to read it if I hadn't a) so enjoyed sharing it with Tim and b) had the luxury afforded to me by all that leisure time.

BUILDING RESPECT AND SHARING EACH OTHER'S WORLD FOR A WHILE:

For me, one of the most valuable aspects of the trip in terms of our relationship was the way in which it helped us to understand the other partner's world. I think Tim had imagined that the year abroad would give him the kind of leisure time he had only ever dreamed of and although there was certainly *more* leisure time than he was used to, he also came to find out that having three kids with you is pretty much all-consuming. For once, we were properly *sharing* the parenting duties. Not just him stepping in for a few hours over a weekend 'helping me out' but him really taking on half the role of child-rearing and I think it is fair to say he found it exhausting. I'm not cackling into my cornflakes with glee at him feeling my pain, I don't say with with any hint of malice or retribution but instead I mean it with true honesty that it was so valuable for me to hear him say, truthfully, "I didn't realise it was so hard." "How have you done this on your own for so many years?" In the past I knew he valued me- since we had the kids he'd been well aware that I did most of the legwork in looking after the children but for him to live it with me and witness the overwhelming, tumultuous, joyfully draining reality of young children- well that was life-changing for us as a couple. I feel more valued now than I ever have done before and that has served to enrich our relationship no end.

IT WAS a mutual building of respect though. I saw how different Tim could be with the children when he was away from the pressures and stresses of work. We had a lot of time to talk about possible new futures but when every dream basically boiled down to the need for a reliable and reasonably sized income, we realised how reliant we were on Tim and his job with all its long, stressful hours and hideous commute. I think I was able to stop being jealous of his career and see that he felt like a slave to it in many ways, whereas he was prepared to give me the time and space to try out new avenues (like book-writing) whilst financially supporting our dreams and ambitions and because of that he will always be my hero.

FIGHTING:

Don't get me wrong, it wasn't suddenly all moonbeams and rainbows. We still argued and we definitely got on each other's nerves from time to time. In a way though, this was still a positive thing for us as couple. In our busy home lives, we would often get irate with one another but then we'd have to put a false smile on our faces because the in-laws were coming/it was someone's birthday party/we were going out for the night with friends/we didn't see each other for the next few days by which time we'd forgotten about it! Basically, life got in the way of us fighting- there just wasn't usually time for it! But I think I see that now as a bad thing. Clearing the air and really talking (or shouting) through our grievances could make life difficult at times but I think it allowed us to move forward and to help change the behaviours that are so vexing in the first place. A brooding strop, in a small van, is a very unpleasant thing. So instead of sulking we were getting it out of our system and getting on with it (for the most part). And I tell you what- I reckon this is the way forward! I don't think our relationship has ever been more honest and open.

I REMEMBER one pretty massive fight, I can't recall what it was about or how it had started but I remember the day. It was bleak as anything; freezing cold, blustery winds, a fine mist of rain that occasionally turned to snow. It was grim. Everyone was in a filthy mood. We were in Germany at the time and I was spending a lot of time on Google-maps working out whether or not we could make it back to the South of Spain any time soon. I considered ditching our big tour of Europe, forsaking it for a year of sunshine instead! We'd spent a pretty cold and uninspiring couple of days in Munich- lovely city but we'd caught it on a bank holiday (as we had a habit of doing) and everything was shut! As I looked on the map at our route out of the city I saw that we would be passing very close to the town of Dachau. Weighing up in my mind whether or not a visit to the memorial site at the notorious concentration camp at Dachau might tip us over the edge of the emotional precipice that day, I decided to request a stop. We pulled into the car park and talked to the children about it a little. I wasn't sure whether or not they would cope with what they would see there (it is not recommended for under 12s) so I decided to go in first, alone and then we could make decision about who who should go in with Tim afterwards. My goodness. It is hard to find the words to express how it made me feel as I walked through the gates to that desolate and haunting place that winter's day. Having been feeling a bit sorry for myself, I took a sucker-punch to the guts for my ridiculously indulgent self-pity. I walked around the whole place with tightly clenched teeth in a bid to suppress the absolutely overpowering devastation I felt at witnessing a scene of such horror. The weather was entirely fitting for this scene of pure, manmade evil. I knew quite a lot about the holocaust: I've seen the films; I've read the books; I've visited museums and monuments. But nothing prepares you for a concentration camp. I had to hold myself together as I entered the crematorium and the gas chamber. The one at Dachau wasn't used on anything like the scale of Auschwitz, it wasn't used to exterminate large groups at a time but it was build with that purpose in mind- a kind of trial run for the bigger sites and to stand inside it was an experience I will be haunted by for the rest of my life. I had to fight the urges and instincts of my body which were to vomit, cry, wail, scream... anything to try and purge this chilling grief I felt that humanity had allowed this to happen. A church, three chapels and a Jewish memorial have been built here but the entire place still feels godless and devoid of anything good.

I WALKED BACK to my husband and children with a heart heavier than I had ever known it. I hugged my kids and told them not to go inside. We'll take them back when they are older- they don't need to know the true horrors of the world just yet. I held Tim in my arms and told him he *must* go and see it. And our stupid fight was not only forgotten it was so insignificant, it became nothing at all.

AFTER TIM HAD VISITED, for the first part of the onward drive we shared a meaningful silence. It seemed crass to try and find any words for what we had seen. We both knew what it meant and we were both reminded of how important our trip was. We were tying to open our children's eyes to the world. To show them that wherever you go that people still have hearts and minds and goodness and love. And to show them that no matter what happens, we must find a connection with people who are different to us. We must trust in our ability to solve our differences with forgiveness and compassion.

SEX:

On an entirely different note, I'm sure so many people must have wondered what living in a van did for our sex life. It's a testament to how classy my friends are that none of them has dared to ask me! But if you're wondering about heading off on your own van trip, it must be something that has crossed your mind. I know it was one of my major fears- that sleeping in a small metal box with our three kids would mean we would never find time for any physical intimacy. Happily, I can report that I was very wrong.

No-one wants to hear too many details but I am happy to confirm that if your children are heavy sleepers (ours are), you *can* have sex in a campervan! Sleeping, as we did, in a bed over the cab, space is definitely limited, but with some imagination and flexibility- you'll be fine!

Actually, I think our relationship was so much stronger in so many ways whilst we were away. Feeling proud of what you are doing, whilst at the same time being invigorated and energised by all the places you are seeing and exploring together, makes for such an incredible level of intimacy. I also think that being in such close physical proximity all the time helped us to bond. You know how you're told to have as much skin to skin contact with your baby as possible in their first year? I think it was bit like that- we were touching and near each other all day long and it made us a better, more connected couple. Add this to a bit of sunshine and a couple of glasses of very cheap wine before bed (you've got to love southern Europe for its supermarket alcohol prices) and your relationship is well and truly onto a winner. Don't believe me? Try it!

CONCLUSIONS:

I have probably gloated enough about all the wonderful opportunity we had for self-enrichment on the trip but humour me for just one more here: I had the happy opportunity to read 'Middlemarch' during our adventure. Brilliantly, classics are free to download on Kindles and I had the kind of time and patience needed to devote oneself to reading such a great book. I absolutely loved it. If you haven't read it yet, try it for your next bit of literary indulgence. There is a great quotation at the finale where George Eliot tells us that:

> "Marriage, which has been the bourne of so many narratives, is still a great beginning...which makes the advancing years a climax, and age the harvest of sweet memories in common."

I must have read that line five times over as I marvelled at how brilliantly it summed up the amazing adventure I had been on with my husband. We spent a whole year accumulating such a wealth of sweet memories:

- watching the sunset together on the beautiful Italian coast.
- seeing the famous gondolas, loaded with Carnival-goers on the Venetian canals.
- Sharing a sangria on the steps of a church in San Sebastian.
- Crossing 'The Bridge' from Denmark to Sweden like we'd seen on the TV show at home (but this time there were no grisly murders!).

- Enjoying a cable car ride down the side of the mountain to the ski resort in the Sierra Nevada.
- Barbecuing sausages and marshmallows by the beach at Christmas-time in Spain.
- Enjoying a night-time paddle on the Algarve.
- Skinny dipping in the Ardeche.
- Seeing the place where the Atlantic meets the Mediterranean and feeling like we were at the edge of the world.
- Watching our children delight in the freedoms of adventure in so many beautiful places.

Truly, I could go on forever. Harvesting these memories, I hope and believe, will keep our relationship strong and healthy for many years to come.

CHAPTER 6

HEALTH ON THE ROAD

"What did you do about doctors and stuff? Did anyone get sick?"

I was largely unworried about our health as I planned our big adventure. I did have a brief moment of panic when I called our local doctors' surgery two months before departure, assuming they would just reassure me that as we were staying within the EU, we didn't need any special treatments. However, this was not my reality; I was spoken to, in a tone of disgust, by the travel nurse who told me that I should have been in touch with them MUCH sooner. She clearly thought I was the most irresponsible parent the world has ever known. When I asked which vaccinations we needed, she was outraged that I hadn't done any research and told me to look it up then get back to her. I was a bit flabbergasted really. We were not planning to visit any countries that I would have considered dangerous or risky. If I was flying to any one of them for a holiday, I would not have dreamed of asking the doctors for any vaccinations. I did look into it a little bit, and it was like most things- if you ask Google about it, you come away thinking you are on the verge of a near and certain death. The internet seemed to suggest we should consider vaccinations against Hep A, Cholera, Polio, Rabies and Tick-bourne Encephalitis. Weighing up the chances of contracting hideous diseases whilst in the safety of the European Union against the enormous cost and inconvenience of getting these vaccinations privately, we decided we would take our chances. I mean, how dangerous could it really be?

BY NOW, in a state of panic I did ask our GP to provide me with a dose or two of generic antibiotics in case the kids got sick whilst we were away but she wasn't having any of it. So I stocked up on Calpol and antiseptic cream, checked that our EHIC cards were in date and kept my fingers crossed as we headed off into the unknown. They *do have doctors in Europe* I told myself and anyone who would listen. We'll be fine...

IN FACT, we were fine. It was probably the healthiest year of our lives. Here's the story of our many ups and a few bumps down:

MENTAL HEALTH AND SELF IMPROVEMENT (YOGA):

Heading off on the road, as you might imagine, we had a world of good intentions and pie-in-the-sky-ideas in our back pocket. We were so desperate to improve *everything* that we got a bit carried away, and life on the road (working in cahoots with the kids) soon showed us what was (and wasn't) going to work. For instance- yoga. Tim had been getting into yoga in a big way since suffering a prolapsed disc about six months before we left the UK. On doctors' recommendations, he had taken up yoga as a way of improving his spinal mobility, but found that it offered him much more than just pain relief- it was also a way of maintaining better mental health. Before we left, Tim dreamed of us all doing yoga on the beach together, as a family, every morning. It was difficult to find enough time for yoga in our busy home-lives but we were hopeful that the open road might lead us to enlightenment.

AS I MENTIONED in an earlier chapter, getting to know the camper van took a little more time that we had anticipated. Even the smallest tasks- like getting everyone up, dressed and breakfasted- seemed to take until lunchtime, and the increasingly late lie- ins were not helping! So morning yoga didn't really take off. However, spending a few days with a fellow traveller who was a yoga instructor got Tim motivated again and before too long he was corralling us onto the beach for some flexing and bending. I really want to be the kind of person who likes yoga. I truly do. I thought that moving into the hippy life-style would help me to embrace the slower, meditative vibe of it. As it turns out, I am just not cut out for yoga. Much as I enjoy the stretching and relaxing, I just lack the patience needed to commit for more than five minutes. After that I am bored. Even on the beach with the most beautiful, relaxing vista in front of me, I start to get irritated by the soothing tones of the online instructor and begin to envisage smacking her around the head with the nearest fast-forward button. It became clear that our sons felt the same way. Our daughter, however, was more open to the experience and she loved taking the time out of the day to stretch and move with her Daddy. Honesty prompts me to point out that she was rather a fair-weather Yogi but it was definitely a positive bonding experience for those two.

AND TIM, well he found his happy place all over Europe. Yoga became a form of solace and relaxation that he could find time for almost every day. Initially embarrassed to downward-dog in the open air, overlooked by all the other campers, he soon lost his sense of embarrassment and was happy to throw his legs and arms around all over the place. Once or twice, a concerned elderly camper did stoop to enquire if he needed any help as he lay, bent double, prostrate on the floor! Even in another language, its easy to understand that the person standing over you has grave concern for your welfare! But apart from having to learn to mime "I'm fine. Really. I'm just at home with my Om," yoga seemed to give Tim great satisfaction. As the person who knows him better than anyone else in the world I can attest, confidently, to the benefits of regular yoga. He was a new man.

THE CURE FOR BACK PAIN?

As for Tim's back, the change in his levels of pain was absolutely remarkable. When people heard were heading off on the road after Tim had suffered his prolapsed disc, many were concerned that he wouldn't manage it. I must admit that I had my own fears on this front. After a bit of research online, I invested in a memory foam mattress topper for our overcab bed which made the bed divinely comfortable and toasty warm. The daily yoga and the active lifestyle seemed to make a world of difference to the man who was used to sitting at his desk for ten hours a day. He was throwing the kids around in swimming pools, hiking up mountains, giving small people piggy-backs and shoulder-carries around big cities, playing stuck-in-the-mud on the beach. All without any need for any of the painkillers he had been taking on a regular basis at home.

PS POSTSCRIPT: The saddest thing I have to report on this front? On his return to work, Tim had been back to the grindstone for just three weeks when he suffered a repeat prolapsed disc. As I watched him writhe around in agony, unable to sit, lay down, stand or kneel in any kind of comfortable position, it became clear to me that our bodies are not meant to endure the kind of sedentary lifestyles we force them into in this crazy office-life-style. Just three weeks of commuting and sitting tensed up at a computer broke my husband again. How sad is that? Modern life is killing us. Tim and I began to wonder why on earth we had come back to it.

HEADSPACE AND FITNESS:

Me? Ok, I wasn't the hippy-yoga-lady I'd hoped to become but I did find an alternative method of improving my health. I'm much happier going fast and I discovered that running could give me the headspace I needed. It was little short of amazing to suddenly be able to run every single day. For the first time ever, I had a second adult around ALL THE TIME which meant that I could walk away from the children, the mess and the noise and just run. Headphones in. Trainers on. Go. I can't tell you how much easier it is to get motivated for a run when you find yourself in the kind of landscapes we were often surrounded by. Running on the beach (barefoot through the surf or with shoes on along the promenade) was a regular occurrence but I also got to follow streams and rivers, jog through early morning cities as they just woke up, through forest paths and open meadows, beside glorious Austrian mountains... In addition to being a great stress-reliever, it could also be a brilliant way of getting our bearings in a new place without dragging the kids off on a wild goose chase! I would set off for a quick recce jog before breakfast then lead the gang around the best bits of the town that I had discovered on my run. Seriously, having TIME, every day, meant that I could enjoy fitness and exercise in a way I had never known before and the experience was life-changing.

THE GREAT OUTDOORS:

As with the joy I got from running, I think we all, collectively, gained a great deal from the amount of time we spent outside. As I may have mentioned, our van was pretty small. We did have a tent that we occasionally put up alongside it when we stopped for longer periods, but for the most part, it was impossible to stay inside our 'living space' for very long and we would head outdoors in almost every kind of weather. We ate most meals outside, played outdoors for most of the day, walked and cycled anywhere we could (because negotiating the van around tiny streets and villages was a major headache) and probably spent an average of 15 hours a day in the fresh air. And boy, oh boy, was some of that air *fresh*?! Can you imagine the good that will do for a person's well-being? Breathing fresh, clean air for so much of your day? Now that we're back, I realise just how much of our day we spend cooped up in the house or the office or the classroom and how much of a blessing it was to be a so free for so long. A book I read while we were away was set in a TB hospital during the 1950s and some of the patients were left outside, in all weathers, in order that the air and the exposure would cure them. I know that medical treatments eventually moved on, but there is clearly some truth in that notion of the open air as 'cure'. Another book I read on the trip was about why the Danes, as a race, are so happy. In one chapter the author explains the Scandinavian ideal of leaving babies to sleep outside in their prams. The very fresh air is thought to do them the power of good. I look back now and wonder if all that fresh air was the key thing that kept us all so healthy. I mean, there were the occasional coughs and splutters but overall, across the year, we were all so much healthier than a comparable period of time at home.

BEING OUTSIDE SO MUCH INCREASED our understanding of and exposure to the countries we were in too. For instance, when we stayed in the farthest Northern corner of the Netherlands, in a little town called Zeestrand, we were out for a bike ride and were over the moon to come across a pod of wild seals, nursing their young on the beach. We stood on that wild, windy spot for ages, just watching this incredibly beautiful sight. It was the most magical experience to be able to share with the children.

On another occasion, when we had parked up in a random Italian town (Citta Di Castello) and we were just killing time in the local park, trying not to freeze, we came across one of the strangest things I have ever seen. There was a pond in the middle, with one lonely swan living in it. A man walked up to the fence around the pond and called the swan over. It obeyed him and they stood there in what can only be described as an embrace, the man stroking down the swan's long neck and the swan putting its head up as though to kiss him. As if that wasn't strange enough, after a few minutes, the man got the swan performing tricks like a circus animal! He had it running, swooping and beating the water on his command! If I hadn't seen it with my own eyes, I would never have believed it could be true. And that was just another day in the life of the nomadic Hammonds.

Another time that the drama came to us was in another stumbled-upon Italian town where we had ended up staying in a pretty grotty bowling-club car park! Again, for something to do we walked off around the little town and became aware that there were kids in fancy dress appearing all over the place. We followed some of them to the town square and slowly came to realise that this was a very big deal. There must have been two hundred children, all dressed in the finest fancy dress outfits; jesters, princesses, king and queens, superheroes and historical figures. They were throwing confetti and silly string and all having a lovely time. We kept trying to ask people what was going on but it wasn't a tourist spot and no-one seemed to speak any English. Eventually, we did find a kind man who explained that this is just what they do every Sunday in Cava di Tirreni; everyone packs into the town square, goes for a drink and a meal and the kids all get dressed up to the nines and celebrate life.

"Every Sunday?" we asked, eyes wide.

"Of course!" he laughed, "we love the fancy dress here!"

I THINK if we had been visiting places from the comfort of a hotel room or a nice villa, we would have been kept inside by the ease and cosiness of our surroundings and we would have missed so much. Travelling, like this, in a camper van meant that we were forced out, further into the corners of places. Through necessity, and sometimes boredom, we found ourselves witnessing the most interesting and amusing scenes. Maybe we all spend a bit too much time making our homes too comfortable? We've seen what can happen when your home is simply a functional item and not a place of refuge; the world becomes your refuge instead and has an awful lot to offer!

GETTING PHYSICAL:

Beside all the benefits of being outside, I think we were all kept pretty healthy by the level of physical activity we were able to pack into our lives, freed from the confines of work and school. There was A LOT of swimming: sometimes in brilliant campsite pools; sometimes in the sea (top tip- wetsuits can really prolong your swimming season); at other times in local leisure centres because these provided us with something to do AND a place to wash! Unlike in their boring old swimming lessons, the kids taught themselves crucial swimming skills such as: bombing for maximum splash, underwater swimming over long distances, crazy watersliding and, my favourite of all, bonkers jumps into the water. Some of their favourite jumps were the 'air guitar', 'banana' and 'buddha'-shapes thrown as they entered the water. I think the kids' swimming improved far more than it ever did when they were working towards boring badges.

THERE WAS ALSO a LOT of cycling. As I mentioned before, the bikes could be a godsend when we'd parked up somewhere and we needed to get further into the twisty-turny-narrow streets of a little town. Before we left, my daughter was a very nervous cyclist, squealing with fear any time she turned a corner, but by the time we got to Amsterdam she was riding down the cycle lanes, sharing her path with motorised scooters and coping beautifully. In so many of the places we visited, cycling is a way of life. The Netherlands, famously, has a very flat landscape and is a cyclist's dream. Also, when we were in Cologne, it was incredible just how many people used bikes as their ordinary mode of transport- young old, fat, thin, literally everyone was on two wheels. Seville has a great network of cycle paths as does Copenhagen and it just felt brilliant to be out as a family, exploring a new place and getting fit at at the same time. We even bought the littlest son a bike for his fourth birthday, halfway through the trip, and I think he had got so used to the cycling life that he learned to ride it in just under five minutes. It was fabulous!

Another sport we took up on the trip which kept us all smiling was kayaking. Before we left, I'd purchased an inflatable kayak, imagining us living wild and free, taking ourselves out on rivers and lakes whenever we pleased. I'd been inspired by our previous year's summer holiday to Norway where everyone seemed to have their own kayak. It did take us a while to get the courage to use it because we worried if we were allowed to or if we needed some kind of license, but after an escorted trip down the Riba (in the Picos de Europa- Spain) these questions soon got sidelined (along with the route-planning) and we just got stuck in. We had an absolutely fabulous time on the sea in the Algarve, around the islands off the coast of Split (Croatia), on Austrian lakes, on the inland sea around our campsite in Amsterdam and then, finally, courageously riding the rapids on the Ardeche on the homeward stretch of our journey. This kind of experience was exactly what we'd hoped for for our children. They would never ordinarily get the chance to go off canoeing, not without it costing us a small fortune and a world of effort (not to mention the Health and Safety briefings). This was proper adventure for them (and us) and it felt absolutely brilliant.

WHILST WE'RE on the topic of adventure, let me tell you about a wonderful experience we had in Slovenia. We read, in our guide book, about a place called the Krizna caves, an underground system of caves and subterranean lakes to the south of Ljubljana. We had to book ahead and were advised to arrive in sensible, warm clothing. Heading up the deserted country tracks, we began to feel like proper explorers and this feeling intensified as we were allocated our cave boots and torches. A small group of us headed down, underground for a mind blowing tour of this deadly, silent, underground world, invisible from the surface. The cave systems go on for miles and our guide led us down into the depths, all the while explaining to the children about the formation of stalactites and stalagmites (boy- I thought to myself- how much more interesting for them to learn about it in this way, I remember copying out old pictures from faded textbooks!). She also told them about the kinds of creatures that are able to survive in alien environments like this. She got us all to switch off our torches in order to prove to us that not one tiny ray of sunlight penetrates the caves. As we stood in the darkness, the water gushing past us just a few feet away, it felt like a very big adventure. We only did the short tour (one hour) which meant crossing just one of the 45 lakes in that cave system, but one was enough! We took a boat ride underground! I could hardly believe what was happening. As if that wasn't enough, our guide led us to the skull of a cave bear. She told us, that science suggests that the many bear skeletons found in the cave are between 45,000 and 146,000 years old. My tiny mind was blown. That's an awful lot of zeros to explain to a child and as we climbed up out of the darkness again I was incredibly grateful to our wonderful guide for taking us on the cheapest, most inspiring adventure ever. I think the whole thing cost us something like €30. I will never forget it.

ALTERNATIVE THERAPIES:

Slovenia led us to good health in other ways too. We spent a wonderful few days by the side of Lake Bled and its more beautiful but lesser known sister Lake Bohinj and soaked up the deliciously fresh mountain air. Over on the Eastern side of Slovenia though I was hit by a vomiting bug and that was a particularly low point of the trip. Projectile vomiting on a regular basis in a tiny van full of your family, whilst camped in a railway station car park, is not joyful in any way. There is no way I can put a positive spin on it. It was grim. For me *and* for poor Tim who had to keep emptying pots of my vomit into the kerbside gutters. Yuck. However, a couple of days later we found ourselves in area of Slovenia famous for its thermal hot springs. Still feeling a little delicate, we booked into a campsite at the Terme 3000 and took a dip in the 16 pools which were all heated by natural hot springs. These waters are all said to have wonderful healing powers, but the 'best' one is the pool of 'hypertonic, hyperthermic, black, thermal mineral water' from Moravske Toplice. This water is untreated and looks and smells a little like raw sewage. I was reticent to get in but I tell you, when I emerged from the water, I did feel 100% better (and it also seemed to do the world of good to a sore that had developed on my son's toe). The waters have long been recognised as a natural source of healing. Another Road-schooling lesson for the cynical!

EMBRACING our inner hippy whilst we were away also gave us a lot of time to think about promoting good mental health in our children and mindfulness was something we kept reading and hearing about. Inspired, and with plenty of time on our hands, we decided to give it a try. Like yoga, we had mixed success with it. Sometimes wen we asked the children (perhaps after a particularly fretful day) to lie down and listen to a mindfulness lesson, they responded well and told us how much calmer they felt and how much better they slept. Other times, being told to lie down quietly made them restless and cross and they just didn't have the patience to do as the instructor asked (I think this must be my influence in their genetics). Tim got really into it, and like the yoga, it became part of his daily rituals of looking after his health. I think this was an excellent thing. I don't think I've ever known him to sleep as well as he did that year in the van. He would often listen to a mindfulness podcast before going to sleep and it seemed to be of real benefit to him. The kids didn't want to do it in such a structured way on a regular basis, but there were times when one of them would flip out and then ask to listen with headphones to a mindfulness lesson on our phone as a way of calming down. This is something I would recommend to all parents. It became a very powerful strategy for diffusing tension. Me? Again, I think I am too uptight and impatient for long periods of deep breathing and mind-emptying but there was one mindfulness exercise which came to be of great benefit to all of us. One of the things we read advised us to focus our brains, at the end of the day on key points and positive lessons to take from the day. Each evening, as we tucked the kids into bed, we asked them, individually, to give us three successes from their day, one 'wish' (something they wish they could have done differently) and one thing they were grateful for. You know how life with kids is- you try things for a while, like reward charts or behaviour strategies, but often they fall out of use because the kids grow out of them or they stop working. That really hasn't been the case with this little aspect of mindfulness and it is something we are still doing every night because it really does help all of us to make sense of the day, process it and learn a little thing from it. Focusing on their 'successes', which can be as varied as 'I enjoyed visiting Pag Island,' 'I ate my tea without whinging,' to 'I think I really helped my sister with her football skills today,' gives them a chance to celebrate things they are proud of. The 'wish' and the 'gratitude' help them to be a little less introspective and to think a bit more about the people around them. The 'grateful' tends to be my favourite as they think deeply and tell me that "I am grateful the sun shone today," or "I am grateful to my brother for making me laugh when I hurt myself," or "I am grateful that we were so lucky to come on this trip." The 'wish' was often also lead to some interesting reflections such as "I wish I had been kinder," "I wish I had worked harder," or "I wish I'd had a better attitude when..." Tim and I found ourselves trying to be mindful in the same way as we lay in bed each night too. Honestly, it is a great way to calm your brain down and allow yourself to focus on the positive elements of your day. It can be too easy, can't it, to think about all the things that went wrong that day or all the things you've got to do tomorrow? Give it try tonight- three successes, one wish and one thing you're grateful for- highly recommended.

WHEN THINGS GO WRONG:

Right, so we were all healthier than we had ever been, free of back pain and taking good care of our mental health. We were active and adventurous and I was providing ALL meals for ALL the family at every mealtime which meant that everyone was eating a pretty healthy, balanced diet. Things really were pretty awesome. However, no-one could expect our year to be completely without incident and there were one or two moments of ill health. Here's what happened and how we dealt with them:

APART from the aforementioned vomiting bug which was totally grim and which took hold of three of us over the course of a week, we didn't really suffer with any minor ailments. Vomit in a van is a definite challenge and I did miss my washing machine most desperately in that week but we got through it. We only had occasion to visit a healthcare professional three times during our year away and none of these were as stressful as you might imagine. My son got an infection in his toenail and when it became clear that over the counter medicines weren't going to fix it, the Croatian pharmacist (in beautiful English) told me how to contact the local doctor- just pop in there. I did so, was welcomed with open arms and they gave me an appointment within an hour to return with my son. She smiled, listened, prescribed a cream and gave me a bill for about £25. Although that hurt our weekly budget a little, I really could not have asked for better service and I was amazed at how much easier it was to get an appointment with her than to see our own GP at home. Now, for some reason that I couldn't fathom, she wouldn't accept our EHIC, but, come on, in the grand scheme of things, £25 to get your foot fixed in a country a very long way from home, seemed a bargain.

Another time, my husband had a problem with his eye. His whole eyeball turned deep red and he was getting dreadful headaches. An extensive Google search told me he was obviously suffering from Glaucoma and needed to get to an Emergency Doctor as soon as possible. We were in France at the time and the lovely campsite owner called a few opticians for us who all told us to go to the local A and E. When we got there, I was aghast to find that no-one spoke English but my A-Level French stood me in good stead and I managed to find enough words to convey my concerns to the staff. We were seen within in hour by a specialist ophthalmologist who assured me it wasn't glaucoma (which in French is, luckily, "glaucoma"!) but he sent us away with some drops in and asked us to come back later that afternoon. OK, that afternoon there was quite a lot of waiting around and it did feel much more like an NHS hospital experience but happily, at the end of it all they took a copy of our EHIC details, smiled and sent us on our way. What an amazing benefit of being part of the European Union. We were so glad to have been given that peace of mind and enormously grateful to the wonderful staff we saw there (I am also grateful to my A-level French teachers who may have been proud of how much vocabulary came back to me 18 years later!!).

The last time we saw a doctor was both the saddest and the easiest. Whilst playing in a camper stop in Denmark, my daughter fell off a giant pipe and landed painfully on her arm. Tough-nut that she is, she took some paracetamol and slept on it but in the morning it was clear that she had done some serious damage to it. With some advice from the lovely owner, we headed off to another hospital, with our fingers crossed that we wouldn't have to spend the whole day there as we had been SO looking forward to reaching Copenhagen that day. Well, we could not have been more impressed with the Danish healthcare system. The staff were incredibly welcoming and helpful. Every single one of them, from the nurses, to the receptionist, to the X-ray technician, spoke perfect English and treated my daughter like royalty. We were seen, x-rayed and a cast was applied all within the space of an hour. And the hospital was gleaming. The waiting area was well resourced with toys, books, a water machine and free wifi. And, once again, we were not asked for a penny. It was all covered by our European Health Insurance.

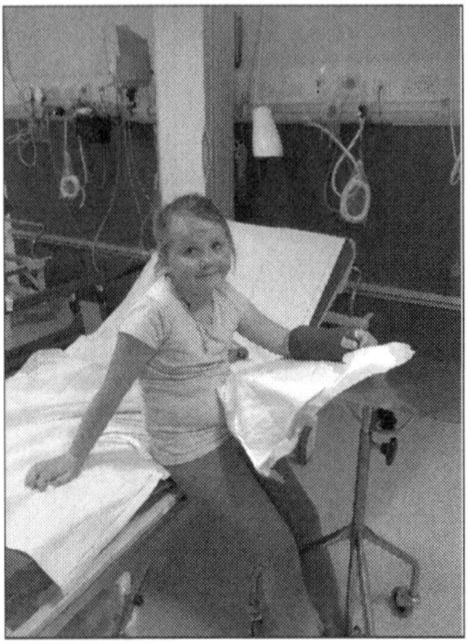

PS Postscript: The arm-breaking incident happened just a few weeks before we were due to arrive home at the end of our trip. The lovely Danish doctor explained that we would need to get the cast removed four weeks later. I told him we'd be back in the UK by then and he said "no problem -just get your GP to take it off." Sounded simple. Suspiciously simple! I wondered how much experience this lovely Danish doctor had of my local GP practice. I called my UK GP to try and book an appointment for four weeks' time (as we usually have to wait approximately six weeks for a routine appointment) and this is when the real stress began!

My GP's receptionist: "Oh no. GPs do not remove casts. Try the minor injuries unit."

Minor injuries unit: "Oh no, we can't do that. Try the fracture clinic at the hospital."

Fracture clinic: "Oh no, we can't see you. Try speaking to someone in the plaster room".

Plaster Room: "Don't be ridiculous- you need the fracture clinic."

Fracture clinic: "Oh you again. Right, let me ask someone senior.... Ok, we can do it but we'll need to see a copy of the X-rays."

Me: "but they're in Denmark!"

Fracture clinic: "Well, you'll need to call the hospital and ask for them to be faxed to us."

Me: "OK. Surely you mean e-mailed? I saw the X-rays on the computers there, not hard copies."

Fracture clinic: "No. They need to be faxed."

So then I try to call the Danish hospital. This in itself was tricky. All I knew was that it was hospital near Copenhagen, opposite a Lidl! Eventually I found a number. Unfortunately, it is pretty hard to understand an automated answer machine which is clearly telling you to press 1 for so-and-so, press 2 for something else, when it's all in Danish! I pressed a few digits and hoped for the best. On my third or fourth try, I got through to someone immensely helpful who found our notes and agreed that she could email them to the UK hospital.

Me :" That's brilliant. Thank you so much. I'm so sorry to ask but are you able to <u>fax</u> them?"

Helpful Danish lady: "Fax?! What is this?"

Me: "It's like an old fashioned machine that sends a kind of photocopy... I'm so sorry. That's how they do things in the UK!"

Helpful Danish lady: "Oh, from the olden times. Yes, I think we have one of those upstairs somewhere. Don't worry, I'll get it sorted."

Truly. I think you get my point. We were seen, X-rayed, treated and waved away in under an hour by the Danish hospital. Getting an appointment in the UK to have the bloomin' cast removed took me, I kid you not, a good two hours on the telephone. If it had been my own arm, I would have removed the cast myself. Anyway, all's well that ends well and we were seen and treated with good grace and kindness when we eventually saw the UK doctor (I love our NHS, I don't mean to be disparaging, but I think we all agree it could be better funded and resourced). As I sat for a while in that UK waiting room, I longed for the comforts and efficiency of the Copenhagen hospital.

So, essentially, gaining access to healthcare in other parts of the EU can be surprisingly efficient and easy unless you have to involve the NHS, in which case take some very deep breaths before you begin.

THINKING OF JETTING AWAY ON YOUR OWN TRIP OR HELPING YOUR FAMILY WORK ON SOME POSITIVE MENTAL HEALTH TECHNIQUES? HERE ARE OUR HEALTH TIPS:

EUROPEAN HEALTH INSURANCE:

You can get an EHIC card and number from :https://www.nhs.uk/NHSEngland/Healthcareabroad/EHIC

WHILST WE ARE part of the European Union, a valid EHIC gives you the right to access state-provided healthcare during a temporary stay in another European Economic Area (EEA) country or Switzerland. It covers treatment that is medically necessary until your planned return home. Treatment should be provided on the same basis as it would to a resident of that country, either at a reduced cost or, in many cases, for free. For example, in some countries, patients are expected to directly contribute a percentage towards the cost of their state-provided treatment. This is known as a patient co-payment. If you receive treatment under this type of healthcare system, you are expected to pay the same co-payment charge as a patient from that country.

The EHIC also covers the treatment of pre-existing medical conditions and routine maternity care, provided the reason for your visit is not specifically to give birth or seek treatment.If you download the EHIC smartphone app you can easily access the information while you are abroad.

Remember, the EHIC is not an alternative to travel insurance. It will not cover any private medical healthcare or costs, such as mountain rescue in ski resorts, being flown back to the UK, or lost or stolen property. It is also not valid on cruises.

It is therefore important to have both an EHIC and a valid private travel insurance policy in place before you travel. Some insurers now insist you hold an EHIC, and many will waive the excess if you have one.

TRAVEL INSURANCE:

I ran into a world of problems trying to obtain travel insurance. The problem for us was that long- trip cover was easy to find but very few countries were happy with the fact that we would be returning to the UK more than once during our trip (we had two weddings and a court case to attend in the UK). For some reason, most of the big insurance companies said a long-trip policy always ends when you set foot back on home soil. My saving grace came in finding an independent travel insurance broker who could look beyond the 'computer says no' attitude that I was encountering in most call centres. He found me a brilliant policy which fitted my needs. The company was called Voyager Travel Insurance and I would really recommend them. The policy was with Navigator Travel Insurance. It was a very flexible policy which we could top up if we decided to partake in winter sports etc.

KEEN TO TRY SOME MINDFULNESS? SOME GOOD PLACES TO FIND SESSIONS ARE:

- ***Headspace:*** provides guided meditation sessions and mindfulness training. There's a free starter program and then you pay a regular fee. www.headspace.com
- ***Smiling Mind:*** This app was our favourite to use a family. It's a not-for-profit organisation that wants to make mindfulness accessible to all. There are

education and workplace based programs as well as ones for individuals and children. You can download different modules of mindfulness training and guided meditations (which means you can use it offline which was really helpful for us). Some are as short as three minutes which was great for kids (and mums) with limited attention spans!
www.smilingmind.com.au

- **Mindfulness Daily (app):** This app promotes mindfulness by giving you gentle reminders throughout the day to stop and take a pause.www.mindfulnessdailyapp.com

RESOURCES FOR PROMOTING POSITIVE MENTAL HEALTH IN ADULTS:

- ***Big White Wall***: The NHS recommends this online community of members who support and help each other. Available 24 hours a day. Courses and self-improvement tools are available.
www.bigwhitewall.com

BEGINNERS' YOGA PROGRAMMES:

- **Yoga Studio:** Tim says this the only app you need to become a Yogi! He has tried a few other free apps but says that this one which has a yearly subscription of a nominal fee (approx $20 per year) has a large range of routines which you can download and use offline. These are varied in length and level of experience.

There are also routines for for back health, for runners etc. www.yogastudioapp.com

JODI'S FAVOURITE ONLINE EXERCISE PROVIDERS (FOR SOMETHING A BIT MORE UP-TEMPO):

- ***HASfit***- hundreds of FREE follow-along online workouts led by a non-patronising, very endearing couple. Varying degrees of difficulty including some VERY challenging ones.
- ***Betty Rocker***- some more great workout programmes. Mostly 20 mins duration.
- ***Ryan Shanahan***- Some fab Kettlebell workouts on You Tube.
- ***onnit.com*** more great workouts.
- OR, get out running. I find **Strava** is a great app to get me motivated -it measures how far you've run, your pace, keeps track of all your runs and links you up with your friends so you can try to beat their times!

CHAPTER 7

MONEY

"How on earth could you afford to do that? It must have cost a fortune!"

IF THERE'S one thing that gets in the way of most of us living out our dreams, it's money. The lack of it, its inability to stretch far enough, the owing of it, the need to earn more of it. It's a bit of a party pooper isn't it?

Most sensible people, in our position, would have looked at our finances and figured that a year of travelling around Europe was not a possibility. We had no savings, a variety of debts, three children and no amazing business plan for commercial-world-domination. We lived a nice, comfortable life in a good sized house, but we were always tipped into the red at the end of every month and we couldn't really see a way to change that. However, I was not going to let such a minor detail as 'money' get in my way.

As we got more and more intoxicated by the idea of a big get away, we did plenty of research into how much it was going to cost. The more we read, the more viable it seemed.

SO HOW MUCH WOULD A YEAR AWAY COST?

A brilliant couple who write a blog at ourtour.co.uk were enormously helpful in helping us to understand so much about long term motorhoming. They've been doing it for several years and their website is both informative and inspiring. In 2015, their spreadsheet told us they had managed to travel full-time for the year, for £12,000 (I see that in 2016 they spent £17,000). Now, we figured that they were only two people (a couple in their forties) and we were a family of five so our costs would be significantly higher. They explain on their blog that they are able to stay overnight, for the majority of the time, in aires (which are either cheap or free) or to wild-camp. We knew that with kids this would be less viable for us as we would need to empty the toilet, do a load of washing, refill the water tanks and generally use the facilities and security of a campsite more often than a couple would. We also knew that the 'Our Tour' guys were able to travel at a slower pace than us because touring is their life, they have no limits on their time and no particular motivation to move too fast. We, however, would only have a year and we had vowed to see as much of Europe as possible in that time. We knew that driving long distances would be expensive (in terms of fuel and tolls) and that staying in places short-term would mean that we couldn't get the long-stay deals available to those with more time to spend in any one place. So, we figured, if we doubled the 'Our Tour' budget and allocated ourselves £25,000 for the year, we could probably get by. That equated to a budget of €500 per week. Another inspiring family, 'Lifeinourvan', who travel long term in a motorhome with their two kids, posted that they could survive on £50 per day, and again we figured if we took that with a pinch of salt (bearing in mind that I think they get free experiences and places to stay by reviewing products on their blog) we could guess that €500 per week wasn't a totally pie-in-the-sky figure. What didn't help was that in the post-Brexit chaos, the value of the pound fell and fluctuated significantly. The number of Euros our pounds bought did change dramatically from week to week but we stuck our heads in the sand about this and tried to just stick to €500 per week and hope for the best.

CLEARLY, £25,000 is an enormous sum of money. I want to point out that is is perfectly possible to travel on FAR less than this. We met people along the way and found blogs from other travelling families indicating that we could have survived, fairly happily, on half this amount. However, to do so would have made this a very different trip. We talked a lot about whether or not this was an acceptable use of our family's money. Essentially, what we were spending was equity from the house (more on this later). We decided that, having taken the plunge and decided to do this trip, we wanted to go big. We didn't want to have to limit the number of countries we would visit due to budget restraints. We didn't want to get to an amazing city like Barcelona and then not be able to visit the Sagrada Familiar, for instance, because we were on a tight budget. We didn't want to get to Denmark and just look at Legoland from the outside. We wanted to make the most of this amazing opportunity by seeing and experiencing as much as we could. We considered that our normal expenditure for a year as a family was something like £50,000 and so to spend half of that, having the year of a lifetime, didn't seem too crazy to us. (I know it will to many of you, but I'm just trying to explain our way of thinking!).

SO HOW DID YOU FIND THE MONEY?

Tim and I considered ourselves blessed that we had met so young. Being in a serious and long term relationship from our late teens, plus living in those days of 100% Northern Rock mortgages with only very cursory financial checks, had put us in the position of home owners from our early twenties. We had generated about £130,000 of equity over the years just from the ludicrous rise in house prices. Now, this equity never really means very much unless you duck out of home ownership and turn it into cash. Anyone will tell you that that's a terrible idea and you should keep your money invested in property but all of a sudden we had a different idea. What about if we invested our money in ourselves and our happiness instead of just into bricks and mortar? We looked around at most of our friends, many of whom have only owned a home for a few years or have still to get on the housing ladder and realised that we only had this little pot of equity by sheer luck really. We could sit on it forever, keep it invested in a house that we were stretching ourselves to afford, or we could spend some of it on the trip of a lifetime.

DID WE STICK TO OUR BUDGET?

By and large, we did manage to keep to our €500 a week limit. When we first set out there was a lot of driving to get down into Spain as quickly as possible (which cost a fair amount in fuel and tolls) and we were clear that we had to get the trip off to a good start. As a result, we were pretty spend-happy at the outset- keen to get the kids on board with the idea of the big adventure. Leaving their house, school, family and friends had been tough on them and we were wary of putting them into a negative frame of mind by being too stingy. They had plenty of ice-creams, cakes and fun activities in those early days and the budget suffered a little for it. However, overall Spain and Portugal were very affordable places to spend some time. Here is a photo of my receipt from a bar on the Algarve where a beer was €1, a glass of wine €1.40 and the kids' three soft drinks were €5 (I mean, the main question is, how does anyone stay sober in a country where wine costs less than Sprite...).

We stayed on a campsite just outside of Porto, right by the sea for €12 per night (and it was six nights for the price of five on top of that) which was incredibly cheap. It had hot showers, a football court, wifi, a shop, a washing machine and a lounge for us to use. We had a whole field to ourselves there and just couldn't believe our luck. Other countries stretched the budget quite a lot further. We found Italy much more expensive than we'd expected, the recession there seems to have sent prices up, whereas in Portugal and Spain it seems to have had the opposite effect. Food, in particular, was expensive in Italy. I had expected to be buying up huge quantities of aubergines, tomatoes courgettes, mozzarella etc but the reality was that we lived pretty frugally whilst we were there. It was January and February and it seems that the food is very seasonal (it is easy not to notice how spoiled we are in the UK in that regard), so the fresh fruit and veg was very expensive and I can only assume that the Italians cook up some heavy meat and potato stews at this time of year because the fresher ingredients we associate with Italian cuisine were rather hard to come by. At the budget-busting end of the spectrum, as could have been expected, was Scandinavia. Denmark really hurt us financially. We had planned to see it at the end of our trip partly because we knew it would be too cold for us in the winter months and partly because we knew it was going to be a struggle to stick to the budget and we didn't want to start out on the trip feeling broke. We had been to Norway the summer before our big adventure and winced every time we entered supermarket (a cucumber? more than £1. A can of beer? £2.50. A small bar of chocolate £3...ouch!) so we knew Denmark would stretch our budget to its limits. Lucky for us, we were well acclimatised to camper van living by then and very happy to sleep off grid for longer stretches, happier to take a risk on wild camping or to go without a shower for days on end. We found the most incredible beach spot to wild camp and some very reasonable aires (though careful research is essential in Denmark- cheap aires are few and far between).

In order to keep track of our expenditure we set up a simple spreadsheet using 'Numbers' which we could update on our phones. It allowed us to make good choices and really think about where the money was going. It was a great eye-opener for us as a family. Modern life makes weekly budgeting very difficult doesn't it? There are so many different direct debits and unpredictable bills and so much of what we spend flies out of the bank without our seeing it that it all becomes rather untrackable. Here, on our trip, we were largely free of regular monthly outgoings and we had so much more control of our spending. It was an amazing contrast to how we spend money at home where it tends to be more a case of put it on the card and hope for the best.

**PS POSTSCRIPT: *We vowed to continue using the spreadsheet once we got home but, of course, we haven't. Life in the fast lane is just so much more complicated. How can I keep track of ever-changing direct debits and the vast sums of money that come out of our account with my noticing? And, despite having much more money coming in, we still find ourselves tipping into the red at the end of every month. It rather feels to me as though modern society is built to keep us that way-feeling utterly out of control.*

Here is a sample breakdown of a week's spending in a variety of countries:

A week in Spain:

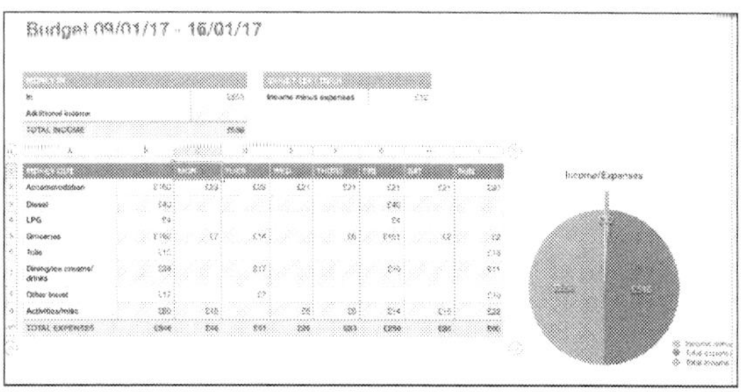

A week in Denmark:

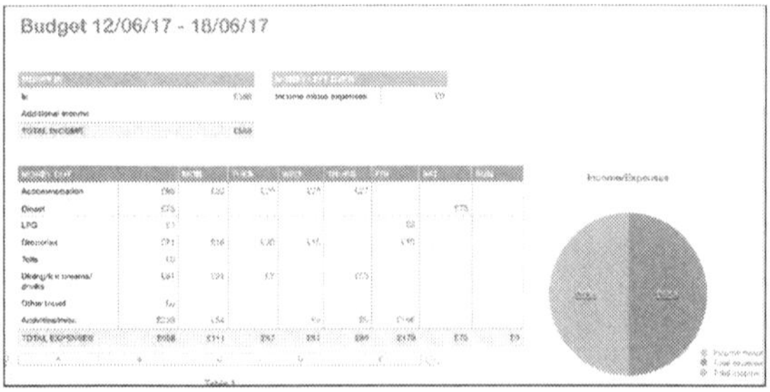

FUNDING CRISES AND UNEXPECTED COSTS:

I'm very happy to report that we didn't have any serious funding crises. Tim and I live in the very fortunate position of having a good credit rating and access to credit cards for moments when we've run out of cash. We were also at that time, in the happy position of having a large sum of money in the bank- from the equity on the house. Some of it had been 'invested' in the camper van (the inverted commas are because a camper van can't really be labelled an investment! Not in financial terms anyway- they are money-pits!) but most of it was sitting in ISAs and savings accounts, waiting for us to decide what to do with it once our trip was over.

However, what did happen was that there were some major calls on our finances that our weekly budget of €500 simply couldn't cover. For instance, we needed to fund two return ferries back to the UK (for two weddings of close family members) and these did hit the overall budget pretty hard. I think, in total, the weddings and associated extra costs set us back approximately £2,500 once we'd factored in the extra fuel, accommodation, presents, outfits and ferries. We had to take the cost of these from our savings, but then, if I think about it honestly, we can never really cover the costs of weddings even when we're at home in our normal lives- these usually end up on the credit card anyway, so it wasn't so very different!

Then there were one or two accidents- we crunched the bodywork of the van a couple of times costing a couple of hundred Euros in repairs, the fridge packed up and we lost a piece or two off the side of the vehicle as we bumped along but we could usually cover these repairs in the budget by scrimping a little elsewhere. I also smashed a floor tile in the apartment we stayed in in Portugal (oops) by dropping my kettlebell. Luckily the owner was terribly forgiving and it didn't end up costing too much.

Another expense we hadn't anticipated was the cost of the vignettes/driving permits required in some countries. We needed a vignette to drive (on the motorways) in Slovenia, Austria, Czech Republic and Hungary. In addition to that, Portugal has a very confusing system of road tolls which link your credit card with your licence plate for 30 days. They call it 'Easytoll', we found it anything but! You have to make sure you enter a motorway via the correct kind of Easytoll gate. Our advice is to read up on it before driving in Portugal. It wasn't particularly expensive, it was just hard to understand. There seemed to be very few toll roads in the south, near the Algarve, but we did hit lots of tolls in the more Northern areas.

I GUESS anyone planing a similar trip would be well advised to build in a contingency fund to cover such unpredictable problems. In imagining our trip we had anticipated that we might have more problems with the vehicle than we actually did. I think the fact that we bought such a new van (more on this in Section 10) meant that we avoided most mechanical issues and we were grateful for this as we read and heard stories of other families being held up for quite some time trying to get their older vans fixed and back on the road again, not to mention the costs involved.

CELEBRATIONS AND BIG ADVENTURES:

Something we found we couldn't really cover in our weekly budget was the extra costs involved in celebrations and we made a conscious decision to dip into the savings to pay for birthdays and Christmas. There's some information on our very pared-back Christmas in Section 4. It was a much smaller, more frugal affair that it would ever be in the UK, however it still came with some additional costs. We sent presents home to loved ones and we indulged in a few nostalgic foods. We did buy a few gifts for the kids and we felt all of this was worth the extra financial stretch.

WHEN IT CAME to big outlays, for the kinds of experiences that our weekly budget couldn't buy, we were lucky enough to be able to rely on other people for most of them. My dad, for instance had given us £300 to share as a Christmas gift. He told us to spend it as we saw fit. We chatted it over with the kids and decided to spend it on two big experiences that we all wanted to do but couldn't really afford- we used half of it to go to the ski resort in the Sierra Nevada on New Year's Eve- which was amazing! We went sledding, went on the toboggan ride and took the ski lifts etc. The kids also had fun on the ski bikes and rubber ring-sledges. It was a really magical experience for the kids, so unlike anything they had done before, and one of the best gifts we've ever received in fact!

We put aside the other half of the money from Dad and saved it until we got to Paris, on our way home. We thought the kids would love the chance to visit Euro Disney- that absurdly expensive but iconic land of commercialism. We had a fabulous day and were so glad to be able to treat the kids in this way. So that was a big thank you to my Dad and a good lesson in the impact of experiences over 'stuff'. We had also been given a goodbye gift of money from kind friends which we used to fund the canoeing trip in the Picos de Europa and another from our local UK football club (where Tim coached) which funded our tour of the Barcelona FC Stadium. It was so nice to be able to send photos of ourselves having an awesome time back to those kind people who had donated their hard earned cash and these are gifts we will never forget!

ACCESSING OUR MONEY AND MANAGING OUR BANKING:

I have never been very good at getting the best deals on holiday currency etc. I am not that person who researches the exchange rates and gets their Euros weeks in advance of travel. I have always been something of a last-minute-merchant when it comes to these things. When we were planning to spend £25,000 though, I knew I had to be a bit better and think a bit harder.

I DID SOME RESEARCH. I read around a bit and asked the advice of moneysavingsexpert. We had a very kind friend who had agreed that we could use her home as a postal address whilst we were away- this meant we could keep our UK bank accounts without any major issues. However, for spending money, your own UK current account doesn't usually give you a very good rate on spending abroad so I found out it would be best to get a specialist travel spending card. What people often don't realise is that if you spend abroad using your debit card, your current account provider will normally add a non-sterling transaction fee onto the exchange rate, typically around 3% (so spending £100 of foreign currency will cost you £103), they will also charge cash withdrawal fees every time you take cash out. In some cases they also charge a penalty every time you spend in a non-stirling currency (usually £1-£1.50) and they usually offer very poor exchange rates. So if you buy something for £5 in a shop abroad, with the worst of these debit cards, it can end up costing you £6.65, a third more than you spend if you use a specialist foreign currency card.

OBVIOUSLY, when you're just abroad for a couple of days and your overall picture of spending isn't that much, you can afford to lose a few pounds here and there, but for us, spending such a long time abroad and spending such large sums of money, we needed to secure a better option or it was going to cost us a small fortune!

AFTER READING AROUND, we opted for a Revolut card as, at the time, this was one of the best deals available. It's essentially a pre-pay credit card but it is a specialist travel card which means it offers a number of benefits. It has a really good app which I could use on my phone to top the account up on a regular basis and keep an eye on our spending. If we lost it, we could easily cancel it and get a replacement which gave us peace of mind. There were no spending fees at all and it offered the interbank exchange rates (these are the rates banks give each other – far better than rates available elsewhere). There were no spending fees at all and we could withdraw a set amount of cash each month for free. So basically, we tried to spend on this wherever possible and use cash only when necessary (which was quite often as camper stops and aires frequently need coin payments).

WE ALSO TOOK out a Halifax credit card as, at the time, it had low rates and no fees on spending or withdrawing cash. We made sure to pay it off in full every month (using our online banking app- thank goodness for technology- how did people manage before?!) and we found it a really useful item when businesses wouldn't accept the Revolut card or we needed to fund a bigger purchase.

RAISING FINANCIALLY AWARE KIDS:

One area of weakness that I was aware of in our parenting skill set was that our kids, before we left, had very little appreciation of the value of money. They were never very demanding or greedy, we'd been conscious to try not to spoil them too much, but we had not got to grips with any kid of formal pocket money system or ever really talked to them about our finances. I'm guessing this is fairly normal. However, all that changed on the trip. With budget being such a tangible and pressing matter each week, inevitably Tim and I would discuss the financial outlays for the week over dinner or on other occasions when the kids were around. They were clearly aware that we were not in paid employment and so there was only a finite amount of money for us to spend. I think this was a good thing for them; they were very good about accepting when we had to say no to things that were too expensive and became experts at negotiation:

"Mum, I know that we can't go out for dinner every day but that set-menu looks really good value. What about if we wild-camped tonight and didn't have to pay for a campsite...could we have dinner in that restaurant?"

or

"I'm guessing you won't want to pay for us to go on the big wheel but could we please use the fun fund to pay for it? We'll pay for you and Daddy too!"

One particular memory really springs to mind when I think about how the trip taught them some budgeting and Home Economics (and Maths). It was Easter time, we had just spent the weekend in Salzburg. My Mum and her partner had travelled out to see us and we had enjoyed a brilliant few days touring the city and seeing all the sights from the world's greatest musical- 'The Sound of Music'. The thing was, Austria is a very expensive country and we had been acting much more like tourists than we usually would because we had this special few days with the grandparents. We'd bought the tourist card and visited Mozart's House, Maria's Mountain, the castle, done a boat trip down the Salzach... Anyway, suffice to say we had bust the budget that week and really had very few pennies left in the coffers. However, we also had no food left in the van and it was Easter weekend. I think, from memory, we had €28 to last us four days. So, as we often did, we found a Lidl. However, this time was different. Rather than drag the kids around the aisles, we asked them to be in charge. We handed them the phone-calculator and told them how much they had to spend. Truly, I still smile when I look back on that day. I had been feeling so glum about having run out of money and saying goodbye to my Mum, plus the fact that we were going to have to 'free camp' over Easter weekend as the campsites were just too expensive (which meant no showers or hair washing for a few days, and at this point I was over the thrill of being grubby!). But the kids dragged me out of my doldrums and reminded me, for the gazillionth time, of just how very lucky we were and *why* we were doing this trip. They took command of the shopping list and the finances and they were fearless in the face of the impossible task we had given them. They thought up cheap meals, worked together to compromise on luxuries and when we explained that their Easter eggs this year also needed to come out of the remaining €28 they didn't bat an eyelid. In fact, they looked at the Easter egg selection then rather sensibly decided to buy a few bars of chocolate instead.

"Mum," the eldest piped up, "an Easter egg, although it looks big, is only 150 grams of chocolate. But if we buy these bars of chocolate, we get 250 grams for half the price!"

What more could a parent ask for? And they were so excited to open and share those chocolate bars, fractions coming into play in the fair division of chocolate (and yes- they even gave some to us!). I think it was honestly the happiest Easter we've ever spent. I realised at that point, that my own skills of estimation needed some work. I had seriously underestimated my kids and they had shown me what they were truly capable of.

UNEXPECTED COSTS OF THE TRIP:

Where I would say we went most awry on the budget was in the costs we incurred in the UK- the cost of getting away from it all in the first place, and the money we needed to set life back up again on our return. I think these were the areas that we had most obviously overlooked (or at least buried our heads in the sand and figured 'it would all be ok').

If I am being truthful, the following need to be taken into account when we add up how much the trip really cost us:

SELLING THE HOUSE:

- solicitors' fees **£1400.**
- storage costs: **£800** (this is absurdly cheap because I found a local garage and paid a year up front. A professional storage place will cost you 8 times this much).

RETURNING HOME:

- We had two weddings and a court case but if you were planing your own trip, I guess it would be wise to factor in the possible need to return home should an emergency arise. The rough cost, to us of returning for the two weddings was: **£2,500.**

SETTLING BACK INTO THE UK:

- solicitors' fees **£1500**
- survey **£500**
- stamp duty **£3750**
- costs of living before Tim got his first pay cheque (no €1.50 glasses of wine to be had in UK bars and plenty of people to go out for a 'welcome home' drink with!) **£1000**
- purchasing new items to furnish the house because we had sold most our things: **£3000**
- All those extra initial 'slightly higher fees in the first month' payments on insurance policies etc **£350**
- money lost on the motorhome (initial purchase price minus estimated sale value) **£10,000**
- Full service and habitation check on the van **£1400**
- full service and repairs to get our car back on the road after a year of sitting out in the cold and taxing it. **£700**
- full new sets of school uniform for all three kids (plus football boots, wellies, PE kits, lunch boxes etc. On the trip they just had trainers, crocs and boots, at home they seem to need twice as many pairs of shoes!) **£400**

Total leaving and re-entering the UK costs: £27,300.

EVEN WRITING THAT HURTS. A huge part of that can be attributed to money lost on the motorhome (and it's just an estimate because we haven't actually sold it yet). Much of it is simply the cost of selling and buying property. But still. I promised to tell you the truth and there it is- in all its ugly glory. The actual trip won't cost you *that much* really, but if you want to sell you house and buy another one, be aware of how much that might set you back.

PS. Postscript: So, in essence, coming back to the UK put us into a bit of a spending spin and we have found it hard to get ourselves out of it. I think we figured that having been so frugal and happy on our trip, we could continue in the same vein once we returned. We obviously realised that it would be a while before Tim got his first proper pay cheque, but I think we were naive to assume that we could continue in the same careful spending mindset that we had established on the road. Modern UK living just really doesn't allow you to live that way and we have been sucked back into a frenzy of expenditure in a way that makes us really rather unhappy. I long for the simple, manageable outgoings of our road trip and wish I could feel in control again.

A CHEAPER OPTION:

Workaway: Our lovely friends, the Brave-Brightons told us about a way to travel whilst not spending money- they use the organisation Workaway.info Workaway allows you to search through hosts who need a few hours' work each week (olive picking/fence building/painting/babysitting/cooking etc) and who will repay you with food and lodging. The average expected working time is 5 hours a day, five times a week I believe (but this varies). Our friends had had a few superb experiences and one or two which were less inspirational-a lot can depend on the personality of your hosts I guess. We signed up (it's about €30 for a year's subscription), but never actually found enough time to book in a workaway project. We had seen a school in Germany that we fancied living and working in for a while but we just ran out of time. It is definitely something we will consider in the future though. You can stay for a few days or for months at a time. It seems like it would be a great way to meet people and explore other cultures for minimal financial outlay.

HOME-SWAPS: Before we took off on our big trip, Tim and I had done a few house swap holidays. They were completely wonderful and a superb way to holiday without spending lots of money. There are several home swap websites out there, we used one called homelink.org.uk I like this particular website as the nominal joining fee seems to get rid of any time wasters. We had holidays on the Belgian coast, in the Loire Valley, France and in Bergen, Norway. I know it's not very British to trust a bunch of strangers in your home but we never had any problems at all. You start by scouring the database for houses/areas that you like the look of, then you message the other family and see if they are interested (it's a kind of weird international-property-internet-dating vibe!). You will send a few message back and forth, coming to an agreement regarding dates etc and you will start to form a friendship with your hosts. What we really loved was that rather than being stuck in a tiny hotel room, caravan or soulless holiday apartment, house swapping provided us with a house FULL of toys (and other people's toys are always more fun than your own!), wifi, cable TV and a well-equipped kitchen. The other family would usually leave out a welcome pack with a traditional meal and an information of the best places to visit etc (which is really fab as you don't just get the usual tourist tips).

We even car-swapped with the Norwegians. We could NEVER, in million years, have afforded to go on holiday to Norway by conventional means, but doing it this way meant we only had to pay for the flights. It was terrific. If you're a home-owner and you would consider it, why not look into it? There are properties all over the world and so few Brits take part that we were always inundated with offers from places as diverse as Oxford, California, Australia, Sweden and the Netherlands.

PS. Lots of people want to know if we regret selling the house now that we're back. My honest, hand on heart, answer is that I don't regret it for a minute. Selling the house was the only way we could fund our travels and the trip was the best thing we ever did. It also taught our kids a great lesson, I believe ,about valuing experiences over stuff and I think that's super-important in our increasingly commercialist society. We bought a smaller house and are we any less happy for it? No- not one bit. It is full of photos of our wonderful adventures and there is less to clean. Even having just spilled out the gruesome details of exactly how much money we spent, hasn't made me feel in the slightest bit sorry. Money really can't buy the kind of lessons we have learned on this big adventure and I would do it all again in a heartbeat. If you want sound financial advice- go read another book! If you want life advice- take it from me-go do it! Hit the open road! You won't look back.

CHAPTER 8

EATING OUR WAY AROUND EUROPE

"What was the best thing you had to eat?"

I think of myself as a bit of a foodie. I absolutely love cooking and am the kind of person who will happily sit reading recipes for hours. Our house used to be filled with cookbooks plus millions of recipes that I had ripped out of newspapers and magazines, inspired to cook something different and adventurous. The thought of trying so many different cuisines across Europe was a really exciting notion and something I couldn't wait to share with the family. Here are some highlights of the foods that we found and enjoyed around Europe.

* * *

SPAIN:

Pintxos in San Sebastian: Oh my goodness! Have you ever been to San Sebastian? If you are a food lover who enjoys a visual array of colours and taste sensations, then you MUST go. It's amazing! I had read about San Sebastian in food magazines and

I was aware of its reputation as a Mecca for food lovers: This tiny Basque city has more Michelin stars per capita than anywhere else in the world. However, a €500 per week budget does not stretch to Michelin-starred restaurants (not do fancy restaurants, I believe, like to admit grubby young kids into their beautiful fine dining institutions!). No matter though, because the food in San Sebastian is also a delicacy at street level. This city is famed for its Pintxo bars and each cobbled street you turn down leads you to yet another bar covered in an array of little mouth-sized treats. The idea is that you have a pintxo with every drink. Its amazing! They range from rustic snacks of chorizo and peppers to elaborate varieties such anchovy, caviar and tempura courgette. They are often served on a slice of bread and have a little cocktail stick holding them together. Tradition dictates that you count up your sticks when you leave each bar and pay accordingly.

We sat outside a bar or two, drinking Aperol spritz and a deliciously cold beer, soaking up the sun, letting the kids choose the pintxos and feeling very, very blessed.

(Ps, If you're taking the train or driving there- don't get confused by the name and the signs- San Sebastian is known as Donostia in the Basque language).

ASTURIAN CIDER: along the Northern coast of Spain, the locals' enthusiasm for 'sidra' is quite something (in Basque it's called sagardoa). We'd never heard of it before our trip but as we progressed from San Sebastian down towards Santiago de Compostella, through the mountainous Asturian region, we kept seeing waiters in bars pouring something into a glass from high above their heads. In a little bar in Gijon one evening (whilst the kids played in the playground opposite with hundreds of other children- as is the Spanish way), we tried to ask the waitress what this drink was. As was typical for our Northern Spanish adventure, she spoke no English and simply replied 'sidra' (with a slight tone of "you idiots"). So we ordered one. She brought it to the table then proceeded to stand with the bottle in one hand, way above her head, as high as she could reach, then the other hand held the glass down by her knees and then she poured it. From what we could understand, the idea is to release the aromas of the drink and to create a foamy layer. It was quite nice- very dry and sour, with a cloudy appearance and a fair amount of sediment. Not likely to replace my chosen tipple of a glass of red, but what do I know? The Asturians love it- apparently, they drink an average of 54 litres of it each per year! It's part of the regional identity. I've since learned that the success of cider in this area is due to the climate; this rainy areas of the Asturias lacked the climate for the successful vineyards of the South. So instead of Rioja, the Asturians grew apples and the tradition continues to this day.

NORTHERN SPANISH CUISINE: We absolutely fell in love with Northern Spain. We had visited the south of Spain many times but the north is strikingly different. The climate and the landscape is so much more verdant and varied and the rocky coast is glorious. However, one thing which surprised us was the lack of diversity in the cuisine. The guidebook informed us that this part of the country is very nationalist when it comes to food. We were surprised to find that almost every menu we looked at along the coast served an identical array of dishes. Typically that would be all sorts of seafood, some kind of bean and blood sausage stew, jamon (ham), chorizo, manchego cheese, anchovies and, of course, the octopus. Now obviously we were not fine-dining, so I'm only talking about the cheaper end bars and cafes but when the kids were asking for pizza and pasta, we *really couldn't find it anywhere.* And as for other kind of global cuisine-forget it! If you're used to the multi-national array of foods on offer on the Costa Del Sol you may get a surprise here in Northern Spain. In a way, it is charmingly nationalistic- it's almost as though they feel there is no need to sell or buy other country's foods, because nothing is better than Spanish food. Even in the supermarkets we couldn't find noodles or Indian foods for instance. Fresh, seasonal, Spanish produce was all that was on offer and it was all extremely delicious. Except the octopus. I'd read in my copy of the Lonely Planet that the regional speciality I must try in Galicia (in the northwest of Spain) was called *Pulpo á feira*; a spicy boiled octopus. So, one day, for a special treat, we went out for a meal and I ordered some. At least I thought I did. What arrived was the aforesaid spicy octopus but it was served on a bed of mashed potato. Honestly, the kids looked at me as though I was trying to kill them and Tim didn't look much happier. I can eat most things but even I couldn't eat that! It was a rather expensive case of trial and error. However, there were certainly lots of people ordering and enjoying it. Maybe we are the weird ones?

Tapas: Tapas is a great way to eat with kids. Everyone can order a little bit of what they fancy and you can just order more of the ones you like and pass the ones you don't on to someone else in your family, who probably will. We found the kids were more willing to try new things in this way when they knew it wasn't going to be the only thing on their plate. We found that they liked croquettas, calamares, jamon, many of the slow-cooked meat stews (the meat almost melts off the bone), garlic mushrooms, patatas bravas, anything with prawns in and the eldest even enjoyed whitebait. One very memorable evening saw us meandering through the streets of Seville, stopping here and there for a few tapas and a drink, then finishing it off with some chocolate con churros (long strings of sugary doughnut that you dip into the very thick hot chocolate).

Bolo Rei: Apparently, this is a staple Portuguese cake but we found them, in abundance, in Spain, which is where we were for Epiphany (or King's Day)- the 6th January. This is the traditional time to eat a Bolo Rei. As my birthday falls on January 5th, I asked for one as a birthday cake. The bolo rei is a large baked ring of dough flavoured with dried fruit, nuts and crystallised fruit. Traditionally, hidden inside it you should find one fava bean and one small prize (typically a small metal toy). Whoever finds the bean has to pay for the cake and whoever finds the toy gets to be king for the day. Unfortunately, poor Tim found the bean and our youngest son found the toy which he took very seriously and bossed us around for the rest of the day! The cake, which is similar to a brioche crossed with a panettone, had quite an unusual flavour. We opted for one filled with cream and found the taste of the spices, which I would guess to be nutmeg and cardomom, pretty overwhelming (but that didn't stop us eating the whole thing... so that tells you something!).

LATE NIGHT EATING: This is just a note, in case you aren't aware- it is virtually impossible to get an evening meal in Spain (outside of the very touristy towns) before 8:30pm. We were quite surprised in Northern Spain that we couldn't even look at a menu until this time. They looked at us like we were crazy people for even asking! I am a big fan of this late night culture, but when you've got hungry kids at 6:30pm, it can be a be a bit of a challenge- don't say I didn't warn you!

* * *

PORTUGAL:

Meat: We spent a while in Portugal and for three week of this time we had a little apartment so I was able to do a bit more 'proper' cooking. We ate less pasta and were able to enjoy dishes which needed longer in the oven or on the stove than the camper van kitchen facilitated. As such, I soon found myself in a Portuguese supermarket, trying to find a joint of meat. Now, no-one in this part of continental Europe, as far as I can tell, buys packaged meat. There is hardly any meat for sale on the fridge shelves. This means that carnivores (as I was then) have to brave the terrifying meat counter.

So I stood at the meat counter. In fact, I was there for a pretty long time. One of the pitfalls of travelling is that you just manage to learn one region's systems, then you move on to another where they do everything quite differently and you are a novice all over again. For instance, the previous week I had become accustomed to the Spanish meat counter. In Spain you must look around and work out which of the confident, shouty ladies were there first and therefore should be served before you, always allowing elderly people to jump the queue. Fine. I tried this tactic on The Algarve. I waited patiently for my turn until I made it to the front, pointed to my chosen item only to find that the meat-man laughed in my face. I was abruptly made aware of my error. In Portugal you take a ticket (you know those little pointy ones from a red machine like we used to get in Clarks?). By the time I realised this there were another ten people whose numbers came before mine. Lesson learned.

Anyway, what this meant was that I had the time to move my brain beyond its frenzied searching for a cut of meat that I recognised (and which hopefully was not horse). Having made my choice, I could now stand and observe the meat buying habits of the local shoppers. Actually, the longer I stood there, the closer I veered towards vegetarianism. The meat counter in Portugal is a blood fest. Firstly, I watched someone buy something which had to be some kind of skinned cat- it had eyes and everything, its mouth was stuck open in a grotesque-death-grimace. I have no idea what that was (and I watch a lot of food programmes). Then, I watched customer after customer buying chicken. Of course- I was in Portugal- Peri Peri chicken is a speciality. What surprised me though was that almost everyone bought a whole chicken. By this, I do not mean the anodyne cream-coloured, tidily-packaged thing I used to buy for Sunday lunch in the UK. The way the Portuguese buy chicken is that the butcher holds up a couple of plucked, but otherwise still intact, dead chickens by the scrag of the neck and you choose which one looks best. I mean they still have eyes, feet, comb, wattle- all just swinging away. Once you've selected your desired Chicken Little you can opt for the butcher to whack it into bits with his massive cleaver (on the same bloodied surface that he just used to smashed up the beef and the cat) and he puts all the bits in a bag for you to take home. Head and all. Yum.

Don't get me wrong, I obviously realise that animals have to die in order for humans to eat meat. However, I was surprised to find myself so shocked by the brazen, bloodiness of it all. upset at myself because if I couldn't stomach the truth of where meat comes from, I really shouldn't be eating it. It got me thinking though- surely I can't be alone in this squeamishness? Supermarkets in the UK remove us from all of this ugly truth don't they? In the UK, even at the meat counter, apart from a few fish-eyes, there is very little evidence of actual animals being involved in our dinner. I found this to be a metaphor of what we had learned in our journey across Europe; so often the continental Europeans were far less afraid than us Brits to face the brutal realities of a situation , choosing not to cover them up with pretty packaging and euphemisms like we do. There were scars of war in evidence in lots of the places we visited and an openness about body image, sex, sexuality, migration and poverty that we saw in different places along the way which was a really powerful lesson for us. I think us Brits need to be a bit less prudish and a bit more European. We need to stop closing our eyes to reality. Exposing and acknowledging our scars is something I reckon we should all do a bit more often.

Cataplana: Despite our rather tight budget, we tried to eat at least one national speciality in each country, and in Portugal we decided on Cataplana: a tomato and seafood stew made with potatoes. Named after the cookware it is prepared in- a huge clam shaped metal dish with a hinged lid- it is a versatile dish of Arabic influence that I would recommend trying if you're ever in the Algarve. Absolutely beautiful!

Coffee:

All along the Mediterranean, if you order a coffee you are given a tiny thimble-sized cup with a very strong shot of coffee in it. Portugal was noticeable though for the proliferation of coffee drinkers. It seemed to be such a common thing for people to do. A very sociable thing too. And boy was it cheap! I think 75 cents was about the average cost of a cup. AND they routinely bring it out accompanied by a glass of water, which means you can sit and enjoy your 75 cent drink for quite a while. Compare that to your ridiculously expensive, lukewarm Starbucks!

Pastel de Nata (Custard tarts): It is hard for me to put into words how much I fell in love with these tiny mouthfuls of deliciousness. Looking around us in cafes, it seemed to be the done thing to order a tart with your coffee, so we did. One bite and we were hooked. They were reportedly first created by monks in the Belem region of Lisbon (which, incidentally, is a brilliant place to spend a day). Convents and monasteries at the time were using large quantities egg-whites to starch their habits and these tarts were a way to make good use of all those leftover egg yolks. They sell pastel de nata in pretty much every cafe in Portugal (they even sell them in Ikea) but the best ones we had came from the Pasteis de Belem- the Lisbon bakery who claim to have been making them longer than anyone else in the country. Y.U.M.

Ovos Moles: Another way of using up those egg yolks, slightly less famous but equally interesting is the Ovos Moles of Aveiro. Aveiro is known as the Venice of Portugal- a small city intersected with a network of pretty canals and humpbacked bridges. Here we tried the little sweets which are made from egg yolks and sugar. The mixture has to be heated and stirred, patiently, for two hours, before being encased in a thin layer of wheat dough and pressed into the shape of a fish. Another recipe from a nun with a sweet tooth.

Francesinha: A speciality dish of Porto. Apparently, in the 1960s a French immigrant tried to adapt his home country's Croque Monseiur to Portuguese tastes. He created Porto's famous sandwich- the Francesinha. Our guidebook told us it was not for the faint-hearted. Tim rose to the challenge-and agreed that it was a beast! It is a sandwich of bread, ham, roasted meat and sausage covered in a thick layer of melted cheese and then topped with a sauce made from tomatoes and beer. Served with chips. Heart attack on a plate; but Tim said it was delicious!

Bacalhau: This is dried salt cod and it was EVERYWHERE in Portugal. I had seen it in the shops but been too scared to attempt cooking it myself; it looked too dry and weird- not like anything I had cooked before (plus, cooking smelly fish in a camper van is never going to make you any friends). However, I was keen to try it so in a little restaurant in Porto whilst Tim was battling with his Francesinha, I tried a Salt Cod and rice dish. Sort of like a baked kedgeree. It was really good.

* * *

ITALY:

As you can imagine, we had VERY high hopes for Italy in terms of food. In many ways we found Italy challenging but the food was delicious without fail!

Shortly before our trip I had been lucky enough to be taken on a food tasting tour of Rome with Eating Italy (https://www.eatingitalyfoodtours.com/rome/tours/twilight-trastevere/). I had walked through the Trastavere with an experienced guide and sampled the finest gelato, meats, street foods, wines, pastas... Honestly, I think it was the greatest night of my life- if you ever get the chance, I recommend it so highly. With the memories of that night fresh in my mind, I was excited to take my family to try some of these amazing flavours.

Pizza: Tim and I met over pizza. We both worked at Pizza Hut in our teens and pizza has been the third man in our relationship ever since. We were thrilled to get the chance to try some proper pizzas in Italy. Not one of them was a disappointment. Memorable ones were the mystery pizzas served up by the chef in the campsite in Pompei- he spoke no English but indicated that he would make us something good. It took a day for him warm his wood-fired oven up but they were a feast worth waiting for. Then there were the cheap pizzas we ate straight from the box, sitting on the street-side in Venice. Then there was the extravaganza of colours in the pizza bars where they cut your pizza with scissors (no concern for cross contamination here- meat, veg, fish all cut with the same pair) and then charge you by weight. All, all were utterly delicious. I think my favourite was in a little den off a Pisan side street. No-one spoke any English, we pointed and ordered and we were presented with the ooziest, cheesiest pizza I have ever tasted. The kids were in heaven, their tired feet were aching from all the walking we had done that day. We washed it down with a beer and it was absolutely the food of the gods.

Gelato: Before the trip I believed gelato to simply be the Italian word for ice-cream. How wrong I was! Gelato, as we found out at the 'Carpigiani Gelato University' just outside Bologna, is a completely different product. Lower in fat and sugar, it has a much shorter shelf life (just a few days for true gelato) as it contains only the freshest ingredients. It is also kept at a higher temperature than ice-cream so has a smoother, creamier texture. We were taken through a personal tour of the history of gelato. We made some Shrb, which is a kind of flavoured sorbet that the Arabs used to make for feasts in the 14th Century, then we followed the development of gelato though a few centuries of changing technologies to its modern production process. We got to make and flavour our own batch of gelato which was completely and utterly delicious.

We also sampled a huge number of gelato when visiting different Italian towns. After our visit to the Gelato University, we did become total ice-cream snobs- turning our noses up at the shops piled high with huge mounds of 'fake' flavour (they will just be full of air- that's not real gelato) which meant that we became much more discerning customers, enjoying some amazing flavours in some artisanal establishments. I remember a beautiful pear and hazelnut gelato in Venice from the 'Boutique Del Gelato' and a Fior Di Latte (a kind of vanilla infused milk) from 'Grom' (who run an artisanal chain of gelaterias) and an amazing Pistachio cone in Rome from 'Fatamorgana' who have a deservedly excellent reputation. If you're lucky enough to visit Italy and you want to try the real deal gelato, avoid the shops with piled high, brightly coloured ice-creams and look for signs that say "produzione propria" (made in house) or "gelato artigianale" (artisan production methods). You won't be sorry!

Bolognaise: Being a foodie, I was already aware that spaghetti bolognaise was not an authentic Italian dish. However, what I didn't realise was quite how cross the Bolognian people get about it! If you ever visit Bologna- and if you love food you SHOULD- don't ever make the mistake of trying to order spaghetti Bolognaise! You will be shown the door!

There's a cute history behind it: Bologna has long been famous for a meat based sauce called a ragù consisting of slow cooked beef simmered with pancetta, onions, carrots, milk and wine. It is traditionally served with tagliatelle, which allows the rich meat to cover the thick strands. Apparently, British and American servicemen who passed through Bologna during World War Two, fell in love with this delicious local dish that they tried there. On arriving home, they asked immigrant chefs to rustle up something similar but the details got lost in translation and our well-loved tomato-heavy bolognaise sauce was born. It ended up being served with spaghetti too which is another thing the fiercely traditional Bolognian chefs are unhappy about! The traditional ragù al tagliatelle is a far superior dish!

Italian street food:

Street food is usually a great bet for a decent cheap eat in most places around the world. As long as you look for the stalls with big queues, serving freshly cooked food, you will usually be onto a winner. In Italy though, the street food is on another level of deliciousness. Pizza, as discussed, is just incredible here (don't be scared by the fact that you buy it by weight) but we also loved:

- the arrancini (deep fried balls of risotto, encasing a ball of meat ragu or a big dollop of mozzarella cheese).
- the fritadella: fried doughnut balls that come in different flavours. They seem to be in particular abundance in Venice at carnival time. The shops were absolutely mobbed with people fighting their way to the front to buy some and we can see why!
- broccoli frittata: this totally took us by surprise but it was one of the best things we ate in Italy. Parmesan, broccoli and egg baked into a beautiful slab of gorgeousness.

Burrata and double fried artichokes: This was, hands down, the best thing I have ever eaten. I did not want it to end. I ate it in a tiny little back street cafe in the Trastavere area of Rome. The Trastavere is just across the Tiber river from the main tourist areas and used to be a working class part of the city. As such, it has a buzzing nightlife, an amazing food scene and some gorgeous crumbling, cobbled squares to hang out in. I had never eaten burrata before and I have no idea why not. Burrata is a fresh Italian cheese made from Mozzarella and cream. Its production is much like mozzarella, with rennet used to curdle the warm milk. But then, unlike other cheeses, fresh mozzarella curds are plunged into hot whey or lightly salted water, kneaded, and pulled to develop stretchy strings (pasta filata), then shaped. The still-hot cheese is formed into a pouch, which is then filled with scraps of leftover mozzarella and topped off with fresh cream before closing. It was served here in the Trastavere with piping hot, double-fried artichokes which simply melted in my mouth and the combination of the hot, crispy vegetable with the creamy cold cheese was absolutely to die for.

Cooking for ourselves: Trying to cook for ourselves in Italy, was not as easy and joyful as I had hoped it might be. I think it was because we were there at the end of the winter and the cuisine is very seasonal. One thing that was a lot of fun was the challenge we had set ourselves to try to eat as many different shapes of pasta as possible whilst we were in Italy. I think we had at least fifteen: spaghetti; linguine, tagliatelle, conchiegli, rigatoni, macaroni, orrechiette, farfalle, capellini (like angel hair), ravioli, cavatelli, fragula... This was a fun way of livening up the fact that we ate a LOT of pasta in the van! The kids were thrilled every time they discovered a new shape on a menu or in the shops.

Also, we made an interesting discovery- Italians do not use a fork and spoon to eat pasta- only ever a fork. The spoon and fork thing is some kind of Anglicised invention (presumably for us clumsy brits who can't manage the fork-twiddling very well!). The Italian guy I spoke to said he had only ever seen people using a spoon to eat pasta in the UK.

However, what did disappoint me in Italy was that I had hoped to be buying up bundles of low priced artichokes, aubergines, courgettes, tomatoes, onions, garlic, cheeses but in fact I found that the fresh produce was wildly more expensive than it had been in Spain and Portugal and that there weren't very many fresh fruit and vegetables to choose from. It was late January/early February whilst we were there and I can only assume that the Italians eat in a much more seasonal way than we do. When I spoke to some expats living there they explained that you have to just cook and eat what's in season and in the winter they eat a lot of meat and bean stews.

Coffee: Coffee is a way of life in Italy and what was particularly noticeable for us (apart from how very strong the coffee was) was that coffee is never served in a takeaway cup. There is not a single branch of Starbucks in the entire country. This is because coffee is a sociable act in Italy. Workers of all professions can always find five minutes to sit or stand in a cafe and have a tiny dark, bitter coffee. Apparently, coffee here serves two main purposes- contemplation and social belonging and it is not something to be done on the run! (Also- Caffe Latte or cappuccino are very much only for breakfast. They will laugh and shake their heads at you at you if you try to order it any any other time of day!).

* * *

SLOVENIA:

KREMSNITA (BLED CREAM CAKE): Arriving in Slovenia, we knew we had to visit Lake Bled because of its reputation for being a breathtakingly beautiful place. What we didn't know is that Bled is also very famous for its cream cake; its proper name is Kremsnita. Oh my- it is SO good. The outside is comprised of two thin layers of crispy pastry. Then sandwiched between that are two impossibly thick layers of vanilla cream and custard. Then it is liberally doused in icing sugar. We had one with a hot cup of tea (without milk- obviously- you can't get tea with milk anywhere in Europe. They think it is too weird!) in a lovely cafe overlooking the lake and we felt we may have found heaven. For the record, the lesser known Lake Bohinj, just ten minutes further north is EVEN more beautiful and much less touristy. Don't miss it! (However, there is no cake at Bohinj so do be sure to stop at Bled too!)

Beer fountain: We really loved our time in Slovenia and when it was time to leave we chanced upon a little town called Žalec on our route out of the country. We were drawn there by its brilliant free camper stop but were very excited to also find Europe's first Beer Fountain. Unfortunately for us, it had been shut down for the winter months and wasn't due to open again until a few weeks' after our departure but there were photos of it in operation and it looked amazing! Žalec is the hop-growing centre of Slovenia and the fountain, which is located in the park in the centre of the town, has eight different beers on offer to promote the local culture and production. I believe you just take your micro-chipped glass up to the fountain and help yourself.

Bread: We found the bread in Slovenia to be absolutely delicious- very much like the bread produced by proper bakers in the UK; soft, fluffy, salted, cheap. Lovely!

* * *

HUNGARY:

Kürtőskálecs: Arriving in Budapest, we'd been tipped off that we must try the kürtőskálecs. It wasn't hard to find them. On almost every corner you turn in the capital city you will find a little shack serving these Hungarian delicacies. They were so delicious that I think we ended up trying at least five different favours. To make them, a leavened dough is rolled out to about a finger's width, it is then wound around a thick wooden or metal stake and slowly baked over charcoal. They baste the dough with sweetened oil or butter so that the sugar caramelises and then they dip it in a flavoured sugar or chocolate drops. It is served to you piping hot. It's like the best doughnut you've ever eaten, crossed, in some kind of magical marriage, with a brioche. Honestly, if I lived in Budapest I would be the fattest woman in the land because I found them completely irresistible. They are known in English as chimney cakes. (*PS. Postscript: Apparently there is a chimney cake cafe in the UK, in St Ives. I am doing my best to stay away because it might be the undoing of me!*)

* * *

CROATIA:

Burrek: Our favourite food discovery in Croatia was the humble burrek. You can find these in all the little cafes and bakeries and, outside of the tourist areas like Dubrovnik, they are amazingly cheap. It is a bit like an English pasty, except that it's made with layers of very thin pastry (like filo). You can find them filled with all sorts of flavours, both sweet and savoury. We loved the cheese and potato or cheese and spinach version. I believe it has Turkish or Greek origins and although it is a very popular street food in Croatia, some nationalists still dislike it for its links with other regions within the former Yugoslavia. I mean, I understand the messy history but I think the Nationalists are missing a treat- it's so delicious!

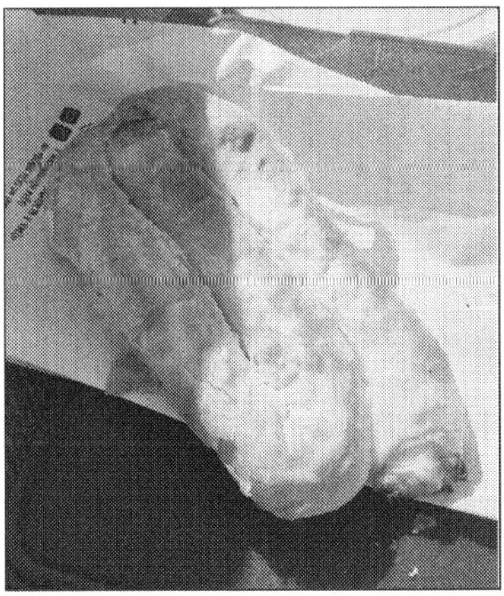

* * *

AUSTRIA:

Monastic meal:In Salzburg we were lucky enough to eat in a Monastic cafe where they served the glorious beer which has been brewed, for centuries, by the monks. In this dark, underground tavern of shared tables and bare walls we tried some traditional schnitzel, goulash and spinach dumplings. All were fabulous. We'd highly recommend the Augustiner Braustubl beer hall where you can get your ceramic tankard filled time and time again whilst filling your belly with some deliciously cheap food purchased from the little stalls surrounding the hall. We saw people tucking into big plates of cheeses, pickles, bread, meats, fried fish. And the beer was heavenly.

* * *

GERMANY:

We arrived in Germany at Easter time and found ourselves in a beautiful Easter street market. The speciality was certainly the sausage and the Germans are enormously proud of their wurst. Unfortunately for me, I had turned vegetarian by then so I didn't sample any, but I can tell you that it all smelled incredibly good!

Lindt: In Cologne we discovered the Lindt factory and museum where we went on a very informative tour. We learned about the origins of chocolate and the process of making it. There's a great museum which takes you through a simulated rainforest, to see how the beans grow and how the growers and farmers live. You then go on an interactive tour of the factory to see the process of turning the beans into Lindt's amazingly creamy chocolate. You even get to try some melted chocolate from the huge mixer- the kids loved it.

* * *

CZECH REPUBLIC:

Bramboraky: We didn't spend very long in the Czech Republic but we thoroughly enjoyed our short time there. We found a lovely street market in Prague where we tried the traditional giant potato pancake (they call it a pancake but it is more like a rosti) with was served with cheese, ham or sausage and tomato sauce. Just what we needed on a cold, wet day.

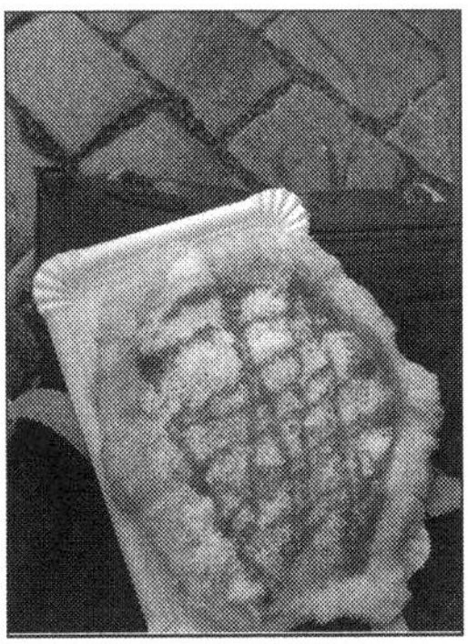

Smaženy: In the same market we also tried the smaženy which

is fried cheese, served on a piece of rye bread with some blueberry jam. I mean, yum. Fried cheese- what's not to like?!

* * *

THE NETHERLANDS:

Stroop Waffles: Since returning from our trip we see that these deliciously thin and crispy (yet at the same time chewy) caramel waffles have been having a moment in the UK. You can get them in all the big coffee shops and supermarkets However, before we got to the Netherlands we had never tried them. We were lucky enough to accidentally find ourselves staying in a university town called Lieden and there was the a sensational, bustling food market going on there. On our trip, a food market was our favourite way to sample the national produce in an affordable and fun way. We gorged ourselves on pies, cheeses, breads and fruits before looking around for a suitable pudding. The smell of the stroopwaffel stand gave us no choice- we just had to try some. We watched the cook squash the thick batter between two hot irons and then in just a few minutes serve us a stash of piping hot golden circles of caramel-wonder. I've tried the supermarket ones- they aren't a patch on freshly made ones. Definitely worth a trip to Lieden just to try them (in fact, Lieden is lovely- waffles or not- it is a vibrant university town dissected by a network of canals which people play around on, picnicking happily in boats and stopping off at the various lovely bars which overhang the water. Top fact- Einstein used to teach at the university there in the 1920s). Incidentally, in Amsterdam, you can get a version of Stroopwafels which are laced with cannabis. We have heard that these are far less delicious and much more likely to give you an upset tummy!

Chips and mayo: Yes, I know you've had chips and mayonnaise before, but if you haven't had it in The Netherlands or in Belgium (see more below) then you haven't had the best chips and mayo in the world. Whole cafes are dedicated to the art of chips here. All they serve are these double fried portions of total delight with a choice of sauces. And when the chips are this good, you really don't need anything else!

* * *

DENMARK:

Pastries: Again, I am sure you have tried (and enjoyed) Danish pastries. Where can you go wrong with a huge whirl of buttery pastry, wrapped around sweetened fruit and covered in nuts and icing? But if you haven't tried one IN Denmark then you haven't experienced just HOW frighteningly good they can be. The ones you get in a good Danish bakery are lighter than air.

Seriously, the cinnamon buns are absolutely amazing. We ate some by the river in Ribe, a charming old town, whose history dates back over 1300 years. It was easy to see why the Danes are the happiest people on earth- the answer is in their bakery windows.

* * *

FRANCE:

Patisserie: You really don't need me to tell you how good the patisseries are in France. Just imagine yourself in the best dream you have ever had and that's as close as I can get to describing the cakes and bread they make in France. And they are everywhere. Every little town has a baker who can make these heavenly delights and every campsite will sell you the most delicious bread and croissants. Despite our budget we got into the habit of buying baguettes, croissants and pains-aux-chocolate on a daily basis just because it became impossible to live without them! Toast and cereal seems so inferior in every way once we had tried French breakfasts. Again, there was some noticeable weight gain (but it was totally worth it!).

* * *

BELGIUM:

Tim had been tipped off by the internet that the best beer in the world was produced at tiny little monastery in Belgium. It was a rather long diversion for us to swing by on our route home but it seemed too good an opportunity to miss. One particular beer- Westvleteren 12- which is produced by the Trappist monks at Saint Sixtus Abbey, is said by experts to be the best beer in the world. The monastery was founded in 1838 in Vleteren, Belgium and the beer is notoriously hard to get hold of. It is not sold to commercial stockists; the only way you can get to try some is to order in advance and collect in person. However, even this is not as easy as it sounds- there are only certain days of the month when they will take phone calls and only a few days each months when they will allow collections! We failed on this front as we didn't have six days to spare to call ahead and then wait for the collection day(!), so we arrived at the cafe before the opening time (having been warned that they sell out on a daily basis) and waited outside, in the beautiful, secluded gardens for the doors to open. In this tranquil and religious setting at 10am, my husband was delighted to drink a glass of the 10% proof nectar of the gods; he felt that one of his life-ambitions was complete. And they wouldn't sell us even one bottle of it to take away- so be warned. If you want to try it you are going to have to get yourself there!

COOKING IN A CAMPER VAN

Cooking in a camper van kitchen is a specialist skill. Part of the reason we decided to buy our particular van was that it had an oven in it. A lot of camper vans only have a hob. We decided that if we were going to live in it for a year, we'd need more options open to us than pasta or beans every single night. So what cooking facilities did we have? We had a two-burner gas hob (which worked as long as we had gas in the tanks) and a single electric hob (which we could use when plugged into electricity on a campsite in order to save the gas or to create a third burner). Our van had an oven which also had a grill function (although both were pretty pathetic) and a microwave (which only worked when plugged into a high voltage electricity source (ie. most campsites). There was a sink which had a fold down top to create the only section of kitchen workspace (apart from the dining table in the van which was usually full of kids). So you could either to do things with water or chop- it wasn't possible to do both simultaneously! In addition, both the oven and the microwave were used for storage when we were in transit and so cooking anything meant emptying said 'cupboards' and piling the contents onto one of the beds or onto the toilet! We did also have a decently sized fridge and a tiny freezer compartment above it. This was a real blessing (although the freezer was never very reliable; it could not not be trusted to keep ice-cream frozen but it did manage to keep chips and pizzas fairly cold!).

Do not underestimate how hard it can be to produce a family meal in this tiny space. It's hard when the sun is shining and the rest of the family are outside the van. When its raining and you're all stuck inside it is a true test of patience and problem-solving. You feel like a contestant in the Crypton Factor. However, after a while I did become quite accomplished and my family were pretty well fed I'd say. To inspire you on your own trip, here is a list of things you can cook in a camper kitchen and I've also included some of our favourite camper van recipes:

Campervan winners:

- pancakes- sweet, savoury, who cares? Pancakes were a favourite when we had very little else left in the cupboards.
- fish fingers.
- pasta- with tomato sauce, pesto, cream sauce, grated

parmesan and butter, broccoli, peas and pancetta... (see recipes below).
- minestrone soup- throw in anything you've got (see recipe below).
- noodles with vegetable and or chicken. Add soy sauce and chilli sauce and you've got a good, quick meal.
- omelette.
- fried fish- it's very quick to cook.
- cous cous (takes very little cooking).
- fried halloumi (but we couldn't find this in lots of countries we visited).
- burgers and crisps. Classic van food.
- Hot dogs.
- pizza (but you can only cook one at a time, which is a challenge. Eating pizzas as a family of five takes ages!).
- thin steaks
- little cubes of fried potato (although these will make your van have a greasy pong for a while!).

Cooks' Tips:

- decant as many spices as you can into tiny, plastic, travel pots. Having a few spices in the cupboard makes a world of difference to the cooking you can produce.
- slice the french bread outside whenever possible! The crumbs get EVERYWHERE!
- Don't be too ambitious. Especially when you first set out.
- Buy lots of tins- chickpeas/lentils/sweetcorn/beans etc. These things will sustain you when you can't find a shop for love nor money!
- Long life bread (the part-baked kind) is also a lifesaver in such situations.

- Crackers, rice cakes and jam are useful standbys.
- Tip all your pulses/grains etc into slimline, stackable boxes (I used old plastic Chinese takeaway tubs) this means you can fit more in your tiny cupboards and the bags or packets do not spill everywhere as you drive along!
- If you likc English tca, takc plcnty with you. This kind of tea simply is not widely available across Europe.
- I found my hand-held stick blender extremely helpful for pancakes/soups/sauces. I could use it whenever we were plugged into mains hook-up at a campsite.
- Ready-sliced cheese is a godsend.

CAMPERVAN RECIPES:

Leftover-anything fritters:

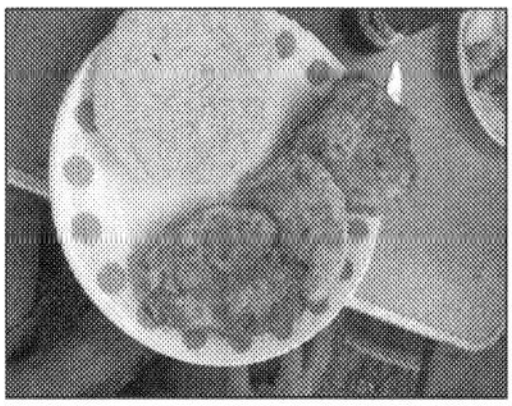

1. Whisk up some eggs, some flour, some seasoning (salt, pepper, chilli powder, garlic powder, onion powder, paprika- whatever you've got) and a little milk or fizzy water.
2. Add a little bit of whatever you've got left over-grated courgette, finely chipped pepper, mushrooms, ham, cheese, peas, broccoli, cous cous, onion.
3. Stir and keep adding milk/flour until it is the consistency of a pretty firm cake mixture.

4. Heat oil in the pan.
5. Add dollops of the fritter mixture (they will spread a little so perhaps try three at a time). Fry for a few minutes on either side until golden brown.

6) Keep warm in the oven, if needed, whilst you cook the rest.

These taste unbelievable good when eaten outside in the dark with some chilli sauce to dip in. Serve with a cous cous salad and you've got a whole meal. My kids really enjoyed the cous cous and parmesan cheese variety.

Lasagne (of sorts):

1. Make a cheese sauce on the hob (melt some butter, add an equal quantity of flour, cook for a couple of minutes. Gradually whisk in about 750 ml of milk, a little at a time, until it is the consistency of custard.

Season with salt and white pepper. Grate in some cheese).

2. Thinly slice some courgettes and mushrooms, fry these gently in a little olive oil with some salt and pepper. If you've got some spinach, cavalo nero or spring greens, these can also be shredded and added for a lovely flavour..
3. Lay the vegetables at the bottom of a small, oven proof dish- we used the camper van grill pan.
4. Cover with half a tin of (drained) canned lentils (a meat eater could use slices of ham or salami). Spread them out as flat as possible.
5. Cover with a layer of lasagne sheets.
6. Cover the lasagne sheets with half of the cheese sauce.
7. Repeat- a layer of veg, a layer of lentils (or meat, or both), a layer of pasta sheets and then a final layer of cheese sauce.
8. Grate some cheese on top.
9. Cook in your van oven for approx 30 mins.
10. Serve with salad and bread. Yum.

Baked Camembert:

Van heaven! (although the children did not agree- the smell of the cheese in the fridge made them moan. A lot!)

1. Unwrap the cheese. Remove plastic wrapping. Place cheese back inside the wooden box. Bake it in the oven (with the lid on) for approx 15 mins at a medium high heat. Open the box, cut a cross in the top and dip in the most delicious bread/crackers/breadsticks/crisps you can find. If you can get hold of some chutney

and/or apple slices and grapes- even better! DO NOT OVERCOOK IT! It scrambles!

Tortilla with anything:

1. Thinly slice/dice some peppers, onions, mushrooms etc (whatever veg you've got) and gently fry it in a deep sided frying pan.
2. Whisk up some eggs (approximately 6 will feed 2-3 people). Season with salt and pepper.
3. Turn the gas up to maximum on the veg pan and after a minute add the beaten eggs to it. Immediately reduce the heat to low.
4. Whilst the tortilla slowly cooks, thinly slice some cheese (whatever kind you've got). Once the underside of the tortilla is golden brown and set, top it with your chosen toppings (we loved cubed feta cheese and rocket if you can find it).

5. Then put the tortilla under the grill for about ten minutes (until the veg is cooked, the cheese is melted and the egg is set).
6. Carve into wedges and serve with salad, bread , coleslaw etc.

Chip alternative:

Our oven never ever produced decent chips. It simply didn't seem to have enough oomph! Frozen oven chips, in particular, were always a disappointment.One substitute we found that kept the kids happy was pan fried gnocci- the long-life kind you find in a vacuum pack in the dry goods aisle are fine, the fresh pasta one are even better. If you heat some oil in a pan and fry those little potato/pasta bundles, they crisp up beautifully and made a wonderful pairing with some fish fingers or sausages! (Thanks to Nigella Lawson for the idea).

Chickpea curry:

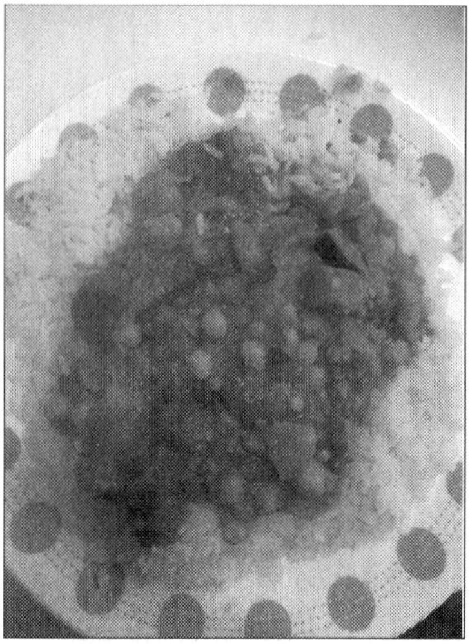

1. Gently sweat some onion, garlic and peppers in a little oil.
2. Add some curry powder or garam masala.
3. Add a tin of chopped tomatoes and then half fill the tin with water and add that too.
4. Drain a can of chickpeas and add those to the curry.
5. You can add courgette, aubergine, potato, green beans... whatever takes your fancy. Leave to simmer for as long as you can wait- at least 20 mins.
6. I found it easiest to serve with cous cous because it doesn't require any cooking- just cover some cous cous with boiling water, cover with a plate and leave it to steam for a few minutes.

Veg and/or chicken noodles:

Noodles are light-weight, cheap and filling. Perfect for camper van cooking. They take about 4 minutes to cook in boiling water.

1. Get some water boiling in a pan. Once it is boiling, add the noodles and cook for 4 mins, I often threw some finely chopped broccoli in to cook with the noodles for extra veg.
2. On the other gas ring, heat some oil in a pan and then add your thinly sliced meat (if using). Next, throw in some onion, garlic, peppers, mushrooms, sweetcorn, peas (whatever you've got). Add some chilli if you like. Add a little soy sauce (and chilli sauce if liked) and a little water.
3. Mix the cooked veg/meat and noodles together, add some soy sauce, a tiny drizzle of honey and some chopped spring onion/coriander/chilli if available.

Puy lentil jumble with fried cheese/meat

1. Chop whatever veg you've got into small cubes- onions, peppers, mushrooms, sweetcorn, courgettes ,chilli, aubergine, carrot, tomatoes, celery all work well.
2. Sweat the veg in a little olive oil in a pan on a medium heat- 5-10 mins.
3. Drain a can of green lentils and throw those in with the veg.
4. Add a little soy sauce or chilli sauce if liked.
5. Season with salt and pepper.
6. Serve topped with fried halloumi (we found similar variants of halloumi in Slovenia/Croatia/Germany/Austria called 'Grill Meister') or serve alongside a meat steak or kebab.

Kebabs:

We found that a good way to ensure that meat cooked quickly

and evenly, and a way of using the cheaper cuts of cubed meat available was to have a few metal skewers on hand in the van and make kebabs.

1. Cut the meat into small pieces.
2. If you've got time, pop some soy sauce, honey, salt, oregano, lemon juice and grated garlic into a tupperware bow or sealable sandwich bag. Cover the meat in the juices and let it marinate for an hour or more.
3. Chop a few courgettes, onions and mushrooms into similar sized pieces.
4. thread the meat and veg onto the skewers and these should cook quite nicely under the slim grill. Turn occasionally. Takes around 15 mins. If you've got a BBQ- even better!
5. Serve with rice/pasta/cous cous/bulgar wheat or tomato salad.

Pasta is your best friend:

Here are some offer favourite camper van varieties of pasta (all are improved by a bit of garlic bread to accompany them!):

- with **butter and grated parmesan** (and a huge quantity of black pepper for the grown ups).
- with **pancetta, peas and a dash of cream**.
- with **tomato sauce:** buy a jar or make your own by 1) chopping up any old vegetables and garlic (onions, carrots, celery, peppers, aubergines. courgettes, chilli...). 2) Sweat these in a pan with a little oil, over a medium high heat. Lid on. Season. 3) Add a tin of tomatoes and half a can full of water plus a stock cube.

4) Simmer for 20 mins or so. It's nice to add a dash of balsamic vinegar and teaspoon-full of sugar but these are not essential. 5) Either serve as it is- textured- or use a hand blender to puree it into a thinner sauce. 6) Add olives, capers, tuna, bacon cubes, chorizo pieces or cooked chicken if desired.

- **Broccoli, cheese and cream sauce**- a good way to get veg into your kids. 1) steam or boil some broccoli. 2) cook the pasta. 3) once the broccoli is cooked, drain it then add some of the pasta cooking water, a dash of cream, a hefty grating of parmesan and some garlic granules to the pan. 4) Mash or whizz it with a hand blender (or leave it textured). 5) Mix sauce and pasta and dig in.
- **Bolognaise**. It's fairly easy to make a bolognaise in the van. It's one pot cooking. You do need to simmer it for a little while though to let the flavours develop -so check you've got plenty of gas before you begin or do it when you are on EHU. 1)sweat some finely chopped onion, garlic, celery and peppers in some oil on a medium heat. Lid on. 2) Season, add minced beef (or pork or veal or even a tin of drained puy lentils for a great vegetarian version). Brown the meat. 3) add a tin of chopped tomatoes, and half a can of water plus a stock cube. 4) simmer for 20 mins or so. 5)serve with any shape of pasta (but do not dare to serve it to any Italians, especially of you are anywhere near Bologna!).

- **Pesto pasta:** An absolute standby for camper van life. Totally delicious, ready in a flash and cheap as chips. Throw in some fried courgettes, mushrooms, sweetcorn, bacon, chorizo or chicken for a more nutritious meal. We ate this at least once a week I think. Leftover pesto is also great in a fried cheese sandwich or wrap.

- **Avjar:** Across South Eastern Europe we found plethora of Avjar. Its a jarred sauce, based on peppers, aubergine, garlic and chillies. There are both sweet and hot varieties. They traditionally eat it on bread but it makes a cracking pasta sauce and is also nice added to the minestrone soup (see below) or the puy lentil jumble (see above)!

minestrone soup: The kids would enjoy making this. Its a good way of using up leftovers and practising their knife skills.

1. Sweat some diced onion, garlic and peppers in some oil over a medium high heat , lid on for five minutes or so. Add some smoked paprika if you've got some.

2. Add some diced chorizo and stir for a minute or two (you can leave this step out if you're vegetarian but the chorizo does add a lovely, deep, smoky flavour and a great colour).
3. Throw in any other veg you might like to use up-courgettes, carrots, sweetcorn, leafy veg like spinach, kale or cavalo nero works well.
4. Top with a pint or so of stock and a tin of chopped tomatoes.
5. Throw in any leftover parmesan rinds you might have for added flavour. (remember to remove before serving though!).
6. Chuck in a handful of small pasta shapes (and optional- a tin of drained chickpeas).
7. sSimmer for a while to let the flavour develop.Serve with big hunks of bread. Such great camping food

Grain salad

A really good accompaniment for any meat dishes, pies, tortillas, curries, stews, fried cheese etc.

1. Cook the grain according to packet instructions. (sometimes easier said than done in a foreign country: generally speaking cous cous just needs to be covered with boiling water and left to steam, bulgar wheat needs equal qualities of water and grain in the pan, bring it to the boil then simmer for 10 mins until all the water is absorbed, similar with quinoa although this has a slightly longer cooking time).
2. Sweat some diced onions, garlic, peppers, courgettes, mushrooms etc in little oil in a pan over medium high heat, with the lid on. Add any seasoning and herbs you

might have to hand like paprika, oregano or cumin.

3. Mix veg and cooked grains together. It's nice to also mix in a tin of drained chickpeas for extra oomph and protein. Another great addition is some chopped fresh herbs (mint, coriander or parsley) and a sprinkling of pomegranate seeds or any type of seed really.

This doesn't need to be served hot so you can get it sorted and then use your limited cooking space to heat or cook your meat/kebabs/fried cheese/omelette/curry.

Stuffed peppers:

If you've got any of the above grain salad leftover, you can use it to stuff some peppers and make another lovely meal! Mix a bit of extra chilli sauce/avjar into it and shove it in! We love the pots of mini peppers for these (we often found them in Lidl).

1. Carefully chop the top off each pepper and use your

knife to carve out the white middle section of each pepper.

2. Rub the peppers all over with a little salt and olive oil.
3. Stuff the peppers with the grain mixture and or/some cubes of feta cheese.
4. Pop into the oven on an oven tray for about 25 minutes, turning halfway through.

Puff pastry tart: A crowd pleaser. We did find that puff pastry was fairly widely available round Europe.

1. Roll out the pastry to the size of your tray.
2. Spread a layer of pesto, leftover tomato pasta sauce or Avjar (see above) across the pastry, leaving a border of about 1cm around the edge.
3. Thinly slice some onions/mushrooms/tomatoes/chillies/chorizo/ham/olives and place these evenly on the top.
4. Top with slices of mozzarella or any other melting cheese, or with cubes of feta.
5. Pop into the oven on a medium-high heat for about 25 minutes. Keep an eye on it to make sure it doesn't burn. Our oven tended to burn things at the back so I needed to keep turning it around a few times during cooking. Lovely with salad and or boiled/fried potatoes.

Filo pastry pies.

Very similar to the above recipe but a folded version. When puff pastry wasn't available, filo pastry always was.

1. Lay out a sheet of filo, spread some melted butter

around the edges.
2. Fill the square with a spreading of pesto/avjar or leftover tomato past sauce.
3. Top with thinly sliced vegetables and some cheese (feta or mozzarella work well).
4. Fold the square of pasta over on itself to form a pasty shape.
5. Seal the edges with melted butter.
6. Cook in the oven for 20 mins or so until golden brown.

VEGETARIANISM/VEGANISM:

Its a bit of an aside really but I became a vegetarian at New Year 2017. It was my new year's resolution. Vegetariansim was something I'd been thinking about for a long time but I had been rather too lazy to do anything about it. There was something about being on the trip that made the decision much easier for me. I guess that fact that we were so very self-sufficient took away a lot of the awkwardness of suddenly asking friends and family to cook something different for me. I was cooking all my own meals so it there was no need for embarrassing conversations with other people about my sudden conversion. It also gave me the chance to try it out without any kind of public humiliation if I failed to keep it up. This way I was able to keep it fairly private. I think I was also much more in tune with both nature and my body and I could no longer pretend that meat was some kind of pain-free product which harmed no-one and was environmentally sustainable.

In fact, I didn't fail. Instead, both my husband and my eldest son got on board with it and the three of us were all vegetarians by the end of our trip. In fact, on our return, my husband and I became vegans. Interestingly, as with so many notions on our travels, we found that we had time to properly think about matters that we couldn't usually find the time for. We did some reading around veganism and we watched a few very persuasive documentary films ('What the Health', 'Black Fish' and 'Cowspiracy') which left us feeling it was an issue we couldn't bury our heads in the sand about any longer. Six months on we are still enjoying a vegan lifestyle and feeling much healthier in both a physical and an ethical sense. It *is* worth noting though that being a vegetarian was quite a challenge in mainland Europe. There are very few options available and, particularly in France, you can be onto a serious losing battle when trying to eat out in restaurants. Even a 'cheese salad' may arrive on your pate covered in lardons! Veganism really didn't seem like a viable possibility when living on the road, on a budget, in Europe. Now that we are back in the UK, we have come to realise how spoiled for choice we are here and what a huge array of foods are available to us. Our supermarkets are absolutely full of alternative eating options and our restaurants are really very much more accommodating of dietary requirements than most other places we travelled to in Europe. It would be fair to say that in most regards, we found life to be better in other European countries and often felt that we would have preferred to have been born Spanish, French, Dutch, Danish etc. However, the multi-national, flexible and open-mined nature of our cuisine in the UK is one thing that does make us glad to be home!

CHAPTER 9

OUR FINAL CONCLUSIONS ABOUT OUR VERY BIG ADVENTURE

"Why did you decide to come back? Would you do it all again?"

TO RETURN OR NOT TO RETURN?

From the outset, Tim and I had in our minds that we might not come back. We knew that this big adventure might lead us to see the world in a new light and may even lead us towards a different life. Everywhere we went, we were thinking to ourselves 'could we live here?' The answer, in lots of places, was 'yes'. As you can tell from reading this book, Europe showed us so many different ways of living and taught us so much about the world beyond our own little existence. There was a lot that we loved about Spain and Portugal and in several locations in those countries we began looking in estate agent windows and wondering if we should stay. Ever since being a teenager, I have loved TV shows like 'A Place in the Sun' and here was my chance to experience it for real!

But its a different thing, facing the prospect of a new start when you're there, in that country, with the money actually in your bank account. It's not quite as easy as when you're sitting at home on your sofa with the rain pouring down the windows in your dreary English street with no possibly way of funding your dream home! We knew that moving abroad would be a huge step and it seemed even bigger once we were up close and personal with the opportunity. There was also an issue of timing. When we were in Spain and Portugal, we were very conscious of being in the honeymoon period of the trip. We had only just begun and we had so many places yet to visit. It was too soon to make any decisions. So we carried on, with Spain and Portugal firmly planted in our hearts as places to revisit. And then we saw the rest of the EU, in all its glory, and each way we turned there were more beautiful places and more intriguing ways of living. We spoke to more and more people who were also eschewing 'normal' life and forging their own dreams. It was inspiring and thought-provoking. But it was also tiring! By the time of our return to the UK for the June wedding, the kids were a little homesick. They were a bit fed up of being nomads. Seeing their friends and having a little taste of home was too much for them and they were reluctant to get back on the road again for our Scandinavian leg. The kids told us, in no uncertain terms, that they wanted to stay put.

Adding to the kids' feelings was our niggling concern for security. As a police officer, Tim had a stable job with decent sick pay and little threat of redundancy. He had also paid a lot of money, over the years, into a pension pot that would be severely affected by an early departure from the police service. We had lots of time for talking it over, and it was nice not to have to do it all in one big 'chat'. We talked a little bit, every day, for weeks and weeks, and gradually came to the conclusion that Tim just couldn't bring himself to walk away from that pension pot he felt he was owed after his years of dedicated service. With slightly heavy hearts, we realised that we were going home. Horrified at the extortionate rental prices in our home town, we did some house hunting whilst we were in the UK for the wedding and it all started falling back into the (same old) place. The dream was coming to an end.

That final leg of our trip was wonderful. It was the experience of a lifetime to see Scandinavia which is just such a inspiring place on so many levels. We probably would never have made it to Denmark and Sweden as a family if we hadn't been on this trip and we were wowed by so much that we saw there. However, it was also expensive, far more so than anywhere else we had travelled that year, and at this point, right at the end of our trip, our budget was struggling. We were in the throes of buying our new house and starting to realise how much it was going to cost us to get back on our feet again in the real world. There were deposits to pay on this and surveys for that and first payments for the other... we were literally haemorrhaging cash. Tim had given his bosses notice of his return to work date and so he was now starting to field calls from the office and having to face the grim reality of shift patterns and court dates and log-in details etc. It was all seeming a bit too real and whilst we were looking forward to some home comforts again (proper towels, not hitting your head when you got into bed... that kind of thing!), we were all also feeling really sad that our big adventure was nearly over.

And I can't deny it *was* quite nice to be home. For a little while. It was nice to have space and to see a few of our toys and wine glasses (oh... wine glasses...how undervalued they had been in our old life... wine glasses cannot survive in a camper van and wine does NOT taste the same from plastic ones!). It was nice to meet up with our friends and get the chance to tell them a few stories. It was also nice to visit our brilliant UK supermarkets and find everything easy for a while- no wrestling with Google Translate whilst trying to operate a parking meter or desperately working our way through all our credit cards whilst trying to get through a toll barrier! In the UK there are no confusing systems of payment in cafes or being chased by security guards because you have to leave you backpack at the customer service desk in the supermarket (what's that about rural France?).

However, the truth is that it wasn't long at all before we began to yearn for the road again. After maybe thirty minutes, people were bored of taking about our trip and were ready to talk about all the same things they had been talking about before we left. Once again we were stuck in the weather/school gossip/politics groans that we had been bored of a year ago. After the initial excitement of a day at school, the kids too started to feel very, very bored of learning in a classroom rather than in our Road-school. My husband was only back to work for a few weeks before the commute and the office lifestyle did his back in again. He was laid up in pain and I was left to face the manual labour of collecting our 'stuff' from storage all on my own. Just me and our beaten up old estate car. As I lugged in the crates of books I wondered what the hell we needed any of this stuff for- we had coped perfectly well for a year without it! It was more than a little depressing! Plus, we began to notice the commercialism of our UK lives more than we had been aware of before. The older two children's friends had become noticeably 'cooler' in the year we had been away, in a way that our children really hadn't. Our kids hadn't been exposed to the peer pressures of expensive trainers/football boots/fad purchases or the latest trends and they seemed a bit at sea once their 'celebrity-dom' had worn off. We began to notice things around us that made us feel at odds with the values of mainstream society. We had lived, for a whole year, out of one small bag of clothes each but suddenly that no longer felt good enough. We were getting sucked back into the drive for more 'stuff' and better 'things'.

It has been a strange few months and we have spent a lot of time wondering whether or not we've done the right thing by coming back and trapping ourselves into the property market again. There's also the fairly significant factor that my husband's job is infinitely stressful and depressing. As well as his spinal health being affected, his mental health is undeniably also suffering in order for us to maintain our position in this crazy rat race. So, we have a lot of talking, planning and thinking to do but it seems likely that we will get back out on the road again soon if we can possibly find a way to do that. I guess I'll have to save that journey for my second book! I feel pleased that we've proved it *is* possible to press the pause button on your life for year and come back to it. You really *can* take a year off and then step back into your old lives. It *won't* destroy your children's schooling (our kids have advanced further academically than their peers in the time that we were away), it *doesn't* have to destroy your career and you *can* get back onto the housing ladder. A year flies by- you really *won't* miss your relatives and friends that much! And, in fact, you might find that you *save* your relationship with your partner, reap *huge* rewards in your relationship with your children and gain enough time and space to open your mind to a world of new ideas. If you're wondering whether or not you could do it, the answer is that you DEFINITELY COULD. I simply do not have one single regret.

WOULD WE DO IT AGAIN?

Absolutely, 100%, yes. It is the best thing we have ever done and one of the things I feel most proud of in my life. We saw a chance and we took it. We taught our kids so much about the possibility of adventure, about the big wide world, about taking risks, breaking rules and prioritising experiences over things. If I die tomorrow, I'll die a happy woman knowing that we followed our dreams.

On our last night in France, before getting the ferry back home to the UK, we spent the night reminiscing and then the children each gave us a card.

Our hearts melted as we read their words. We felt like the luckiest people on earth.

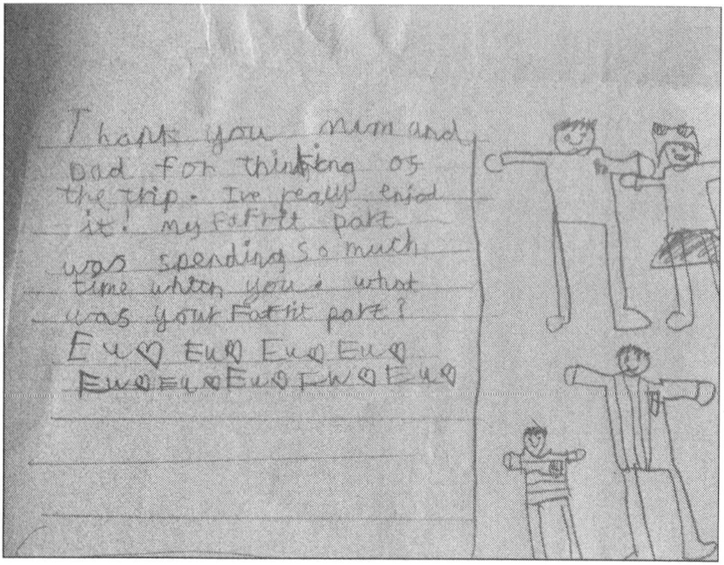

WOULD WE CHANGE ANYTHING?

Maybe a few minor things. We might buy a different van, we might do the course that meant we could drive a bigger vehicle, we might have not chosen to come back. But these are not big things. It is true to say that there were times when I wish we had stayed a little longer and travelled a little slower. We covered a LOT of miles and saw a LOT of Europe, but we also came away with the feeling that there was lots we had missed. We wore ourselves out a bit by being constantly on the move. I don't regret the way we did it; we set out with a mission to show our kids as many EU countries as we could and we achieved our goal. They are SO proud to tell people that they visited 19 COUNTRIES in ONE YEAR! However, if we get the chance to head off again, we will go much slower. We will stop for longer, rest more and really get to see and experience a place, by living in it and properly exploring it, rather than just skimming the surface. All we need to do now is decide where to go and work out how to find the money to fund it... but I have never let a little problem like money stop me before! We'll work something out! Watch this space!

CHAPTER 10

OUR TOP TEN(S) OF FAMILY-FRIENDLY PLACES TO VISIT AROUND EUROPE

"We can't possibly do what you did- but is there a place you'd recommend that we could visit for a short break?"

Many of our favourite spots were places that we wild-camped or free-camped but if you are setting out on a proper holiday then you'll most likely be wanting some luxuries and the security of a reservation. Here are our top ten *proper* campsites where you can have a wonderful family vacation:

TOP TEN FAMILY CAMPSITES

1. Turiscampo, Algarve, Portugal: This place has the most incredible bathroom facilities. Luxurious, hot and very private showers plus a separate kids' bathroom with baths, small showers and tiny toilets-all of which were immaculately clean. There was a SUPERB outdoor pool (which was a bit cold in the winter) and a large outdoor jacuzzi which you can actually swim in (which was open all year round and plenty warm enough for us in November). There was also a fabulous astroturf football pitch, table tennis tables, a well stocked shop, nice restaurant/bar and lots of activities (language lessons etc). There were also a few good playgrounds. A quick car ride (or 20 min walk) would get you to Playa de la Luz- a terrific beach and very pleasant tourist town with plenty of restaurants/takeaways etc https://www.turiscampo.com/en

2. La Marina, Elche, Spain: The BEST waterpark of any campsite we stayed in. Several outdoors water slides and pools with a swim up bar. There is also a family-friendly spa with several more pools (including one full of lemons), jacuzzis, steam room, sauna etc with lovey changing rooms. There is a good sized soft play area and games room for kids, a superb kids' club (and lots of other organised activities such as shanty choir and cinema). There is a HUGE multi sports area for football/basketball/tennis etc and some good table tennis tables. The onsite shop is the best one we found anywhere around Europe. It had an enormous selection of well-priced goods. There is also a nice restaurant and a lively take-away. You can stroll or cycle to the nice beach in just a few minutes and you can hire go-karts on site. It is a big campsite and the pitches are generally pretty tightly packed in but the facilities are incredible. http://www.lamarinaresort.com/en/

3. Camping Les Coudoulets, Ardeche, France: This was a real favourite for us. The pitches were huge so we felt like we had much more privacy than at some of the other family-style campsites we stayed in. The toilet facilities were nice and there was a family wash room with clown-toilets and showers (which the kids loved!). There is an indoor pool with exercise bikes set into the water (!) and an outdoor pool complex including a lovely safe slide/fountain/play area for little ones. There was a games area and a bouncy castle next to the table tennis tables (perfect for us- the adults could battle it out on the ping pong tables whilst the kids played on the climbing frame and bouncy castle). Good bar and take-away and lovely fresh daily bakery deliveries (so you can order your bread and pastries each morning). The Ardeche river runs through the campsite so you can access the river directly (and I think swim in in during the summer months- we took the canoe out on it and had a lot of fun). The couple who run it were absolutely delightful and couldn't do enough for us. There is also loads to do and see in the surrounding area. It's a gorgeous part of France. http://www.coudoulets.com/en/

4. Camping Šimuni- Pag Island- Croatia: This place felt WAY off the beaten track. It is, however, the easiest of the Croatian islands to reach because there is a bridge which you can drive across from the mainland (which is why we chose it). Pag is famous for lace-making and sheep's milk cheese (paski sur) and as we drove across the desolate, windy, landscape we could see nothing but dry stone walls and sheep for miles and miles. However, when we arrived at Camping Simuni we felt we may just have found paradise. This resort is VAST and the facilities are amazing. There are several beautiful beaches, sports pitches, a host of on site restaurants/takeaways and some beach-front pitches with views to die for. The sanitary block was also very modern and well-equipped. Unfortunately for us, we were there very much out of season, and most things were closed. In fact it was a little bit spooky given the size of the site and the scarcity of other campers. However, we still had a wonderful few days playing in the huge rock pools and enjoying peaceful and glorious walks along the sea to the little village of Simuni. We had never seen such clear, sparkling seas and although it was a little too cold for swimming when we were there in April, it was very obvious to us that if we had visited in the summer season that we would probably never have wanted to leave. If you look at the website you can see that summer offers all kinds of water based activities, kids's clubs and events. It is one of the campsites I would definitely like to return to. https://www.camping-simuni.hr/en/

5. Camping Split (Croatia): A little further down the Croatian coast we chanced upon Camping Split in Stobreĉ and we liked is so much that we went back for a second stay on our way back up the coast after Dubrovnik. Here, we scored a beach-side pitch with spectacular views of the sea from our breakfast table and incredible sunsets to watch at the days' end. The site is situated on a little bay, just outside of Split (you can get the bus into town with minimum fuss) and the water is clear, sparkly and deliciously shallow (which meant the kids could play happily and safely for hours). There was a lovely restaurant and bar on site with very reasonably priced food (and takeaway pizzas) and there was a great little town just a few minutes' walk away with lots of other shops and bars plus a wonderful bakery.

There were some fabulous places to walk and run along the craggy waterfronts and it really was a spectacular area. Whilst we were there, the campsite was building a spa which was set to have several outdoor pools, right on the beach front, so I'm sure this place will be brimming with visitors this summer. Highly recommended. https://www.campingsplit.com

6. Camp Zagreb (Croatia) This little gem of a campsite was one of the cheapest we stayed in on our trip, yet definitely one of the best. Situated on a small lake, just outside the capital city (you can take the train into town without too many problems), we had lovely views and there was a great run/bike ride around the lake on footpaths- perfect for a young family. There was a beautifully furnished and tastefully decorated bar and restaurant on site which served AMAZING pizzas at incredibly good prices. They also played excellent music! The top floor of the restaurant/bar had been converted into a mini spa-retreat. We hired the whole thing (huge jacuzzi with massive flat screen tv, shower, lounge, steam room) to ourselves for a pittance (I think it was €30 for three hours) and had a very welcome chill out (no- we didn't take the kids...we split the time between us and had some very welcome alone time- yay!). There was also a huge play area for the kids right next to the bar and the bathrooms were lovely- clean and modern. We only intended to stay for one night and I think we ended up staying for a week. What a great place! **http://www.campzagreb.com/en/**

7. Camping De Badhoeve: Amsterdam: This is a funny recommendation because in many ways this campsite was a bit tired and shabby. However, we had such a lovely time and much of that stemmed from the fact that, again, we had a waterside pitch so that the views we got from just sitting by our van were sensational. The campsite sits on a tiny patch of land between two enormous lakes and we could take our inflatable canoe straight out onto the water which was a lovely, calm expanse- we could paddle about on it without any sense of danger. The campsite owner was hilarious- he was very flexible on the price-

waving his hand at the ridiculous idea of paying for the kids (which was a refreshing change- the prices for the kids in campsites can vary SO much) and there was a nice little play area for the kids. We were startled by the contrast to the neatly manicured French campsites we had stayed in. Here, in Holland, there seemed to be much less focus on barriers between campers and a much more laissez faire approach to pitches, rules and regulations! The reason I liked the place so much stemmed from its lovely location on a kind of lagoon. I went for a bike ride along a strip of land that had fantastic views, on both sides across the water and the area was home to lots of interesting sea birds. The other thing that was great was that you could cycle directly into Amsterdam- you could take the cycle highway down to the ferry port and then take a quick water taxi over to the city centre. A very chilled out way to visit a bustling city. http://www.campingdebadhoeve.nl/?lang=en

8. Camping A Vouga (Northern Spain): This is another example of a campsite that was pretty shabby round the edges but its beachfront location again brought us so much joy we could absolutely ignore the tired old shower block and lack of play area. Who needs a playground when you're camped pretty much ON the beach? If you're lucky enough to nab one of the beach-front pitches here (and there are about twelve), you won't want for anything else. The beach is beautiful, rock pools are plentiful and full of life and just a short walk along the seaside boardwalk takes you to a sweet little town where you can hire pedalos etc. (and there's good playground). A slightly longer walk (or a short bus ride) will see you in a nice town called Muros where you can sit and people-watch in some charming, traditional bars whilst you enjoy some typical Northern Spanish cuisine. Be sure to try the octopus! During our stay here we chatted with lots of other campers who all reported having seen dolphins, on a regular basis, swimming and playing in the sea near the campsite. They kept saying how unusual it was that the week we stayed, the dolphins hadn't been out playing- gutting for us but an incentive to return so that we can spot them next time! I believe this area of the coast is renowned for dolphin spotting so if you go, do take your binoculars! There is also a lovely large family room (which we used for lessons) and decent wifi. Great views from the restaurant too (although the food was a little too pricey for us, the drinks were deliciously cheap). http://campingvouga.wixsite.com/a-vouga/environment

9. Villagio Venezia, Venice, Italy: This one gets a mention because the showers and bathrooms are OUT OF THIS WORLD (and this stuff matters when you shower fairly

infrequently and sometimes in pretty gross places!). The newly refurbished bathrooms were so deluxe- spacious, lovely decor, radiators to keep the room warm, unlimited hot water. Oh, they made my husband and I so happy. I think we had three showers each, per day! It was also a terrific location- we could get the bus into the centre of Venice very easily and there was a huge park next door to the campsite which had superb play areas (including a fun spaghetti-junction-style bike track for kids) . It is a great space which is used by lots of runners and walkers. The campsite cafe looked lovely too and there was a nice indoor pool which was lit, in the evening, by underwear disco lights which made for a fun experience for the kids- a disco swim!! **http://www.veneziavillage.it**

10. Picos de Europa Campsite, Northern Spain: This campsite is another that is a little rough around the edges but we had a fabulous time. The Picos de Europa is a gorgeous stretch of mountains along the Northern coast of Spain and you can enjoy skiing in the winter and all sorts of mountain pursuits in the summer. The walking is fabulous as are the canoeing/kayaking opportunities on the Sella river. This campsite has a lovey green, expansive area for camping (which we had all to ourselves in October) and the children played in the stream ,next to our pitch, having a lovely time building a dam and splashing about in their wellies. The restaurant was brilliant and had a lovely roaring log fire which we really enjoyed. There were also some big trampolines for the kids to play on and a small outdoor pool (which wasn't open off-season). We thought the location was great; there is so much to see and do in this area. The local tourist town- Cangas De Onis is deliciously welcoming and you can't walk more than a few paces without tripping over another outdoor pursuits company who would love to take you out on the river or off on a quad bike etc.

Covodonga is a very special place for the Spanish (see previous entry under Roadschooling) and this is just a short drive away from the campsite. You can also visit some pretty small, but very cool caves, just a two minute walk from the campsite. We got our own private tour, for next to no money and it was a brilliant way for the kids to learn about early man and prehistoric beasts. http://www.picos-europa.com/interior.php?id=7

11. ** (OK, this is supposed to be a top ten but I just couldn't leave this one out!) La Paz, Northern Spain: I read about this place in a Guardian article about campsites with the best views in Europe. It did not disappoint. As we edged our heavy van up the winding approach to the pitch I did wonder if we might not survive the experience, but the views made it all worth it. We perched right on the edge of the cliff face, and looked down on the campsite's own private beach (which we could gambol down to in just a minute or two) and out across the Atlantic. I really never wanted to leave. The sunsets were just incredible. The campsite is well situated for exploring lot of nice towns along this stretch of coast (we particularly liked Ribadesella) plus some spectacular natural springs too. There was a lovely bar/restaurant with sensational vistas which sold a few basic supplies and delicious daily bread. The shower block was about a hundred years old but the water was hot and with views like that we really didn't care! I believe dolphin spotting is a regular occurrence here too- we didn't see any though- of course! **http://www.campinglapaz.com**

PS Postscript: Honestly, it was very difficult to come up with this list because so many of the campsites we stayed in were wonderful in different ways. You can find a full list of all the places we stayed (campsites, free stops and camper stops) on our website at http://www.psweloveu.com/where-have-we-been.html

IF YOU ARE EXPERIENCED campers and a bit braver about staying off the tourist trail (or if, like us, you need to travel on a budget) here's the details of our favourite budget overnight locations. Please bear in mind that situations might alter with these places. Laws and regulations can change/be enforced more strictly at different times of the year, businesses change their costs etc. Use this as just a guide.

We relied heavily on two resources for finding cheap and free places to stay: a book called 'Camper stop Europe' which lists hundreds of places to stay for free or very cheaply (in a motorhome) by A.E.M. van den Dobbelsteen and an app called 'Park for the Night' which has user tips and reviews. Remember- you will usually only be tolerated if you are in a motorhome. Different laws apply to caravans (see section in the Appendix on 'What is an Aire?')

TOP TEN CHEAP OR FREE CAMPER STOPS

1. Lemvig beach, Denmark: This was the MOST beautiful place that we stayed in our whole year abroad. We camped pretty much ON this isolated, windswept, endless expanse of beach. There were miles of gorgeous, flat sand and lovely shallow waters. The beaches were backed by sand dunes which the kids happily threw themselves off for hours and there was a (cold) beach shower and a toilet block. There were also some fun huts up in the dunes which I believe are quite a feature of the Danish coast; low-level wooden shelters for people to camp out in for free. There was even a fire pit there for anyone to use. You've got to love the Danish way of life! We found this spot at the end of our big adventure when we were much braver about wild camping. Although there were signs up saying 'no camping', we spoke to other people staying there in vans who said they had been there for weeks with no problems. I expect it's seasonal thing- we were there in Spring so we weren't causing any problems. It was pretty out of the way and isolated- there was nowhere nearby to buy any provisions but we had stocked up recently and were very happy to bed down and enjoy the surroundings for a few days. Honestly, I could have stayed for a week! n56.47596 E8.12477.

2. Frexulfre (Northern Spain): Our first wild camping spot and one of our all-time favourites! We were nervous because we'd read that wild camping is not very widely tolerated in Spain but a few other vans of surfers and hippies put our minds at rest and said they'd been there for several nights with no problems. It was in an isolated car park, right in the middle of a pine forest (wonderful smell but terrible for mosquitoes!), next to the most rugged and gloriously windswept beach we've ever seen. We had a lovey evening playing games on the beach, feeling as free as the birds and were inspired to wild camp a bit more often. **N43.55986913971805 W6.674022674560547**

3. Seville Los Remedios (camper stop): This was one of the best located camper stops that we found on our trip. We could simply walk 5 minutes across the bridge to the Plaza de

Espana- right in the middle of the city. It was only €10 per night and it was manned, round the clock, by a security guard. Cheap, safe, central- you can't get better than that! **N37.37235 w5.99444**

4. Diano Marina, Al Rosetto camper stop (Italy): Having just driven through Monaco, we happened upon this lovely little camper stop just inside the Italian border which was situated in the back of a garden centre. It had fab showers, washing machines (always a bonus), a nice family play room with toys (and wifi) and a field for dogs and energetic kids. Just a short walk away was a sweet seaside town. The garden centre also sold great bread and fresh fruits/vegetables. **N43.91983 e8.07733**

5. **Lake Bled (gravel car park near the ice hockey stadium), Slovenia**. We had booked into what turned out to the an awful (and very expensive) campsite at Lake Bled, which we left in disgust! However, as it was off season, we really couldn't find anywhere else that was open. In desperation we turned to the man in the hut of the gravel car park, right next to the lake and asked if could stay there overnight. He agreed and charged us €5. It was an amazing location- we could see Lake Bled from the van, there were public toilets nearby and we happily whiled away the hours in this charming little town. You'd pay a fortune to stay that close to the lake in a hotel; sometimes things just work out better than planned!

6. Ribe, Denmark: My husband is a BIG fan of the Vikings. He loves anything to do with those historic Nordic raiders. Ever since we'd come up with the idea of touring Europe he had been hoping to engage in some serious Viking history. After some research we'd found out about the Viking centre in Ribe where you could get an 'authentic living Viking experience' (see section below on 'Best cultural experiences with kids'). The only problem was that Denmark was cripplingly expensive and there were almost no free places to stay. Imagine our surprise to find that one of the only legal camper stops in Denmark was, in fact, in Ribe itself. It was just a big car park but it was a totally fabulous location- we could walk easily into the beautiful, historic town of Ribe with its collection of AMAZING bakcries and well preserved buildings (it is the oldest extant town in Denmark) and there were lots of other friendly van-dwellers staying there too so it didn't feel creepy or vulnerable (as some camper stops do). There were even some picnic benches and toilets for our use. Perfect! **N53.32480 E8.75740**

7. Passau, Germany: We had never heard of Passau- we were just looking for a place to stay en route from Munich to the Czech Republic but what a lovely surprise this town was. We found a fabulous camper stop, right by the river (with a great big playground and clean toilets), opposite a good bakers and just a short walk into what turned out to be one of our favourite towns. Passau is situated at the borders of Germany, Austria and the Czech Republic and there are three main rivers which converge here (it is also known as 'the city of three rivers'). There were plenty of things to see and do, including some lovely traditional bells on the tower at the Rathaus and the second biggest church organ in the world! **N48.57818, E13.47366**

8. Disneyland Paris, Coupvray, France: Now, who'd have thought that this bland, enormous, concrete car park would get a place on my top ten list? Well, this one wins for money-saving, convenience and fireworks! Did you know that a whole family can stay INSIDE the Eurodisney resort for €35? This is a flat rate for one day, which allows you to stay overnight. There are camper stop facilities like water and drainage and there are even a few (fairly basic) showers in the toilet block. You can literally walk into the park and at the end of the night you can sit back watch the fireworks from the comfort of your motorhome, beer in hand after a tough day on the rides! This was by FAR the easiest and cheapest way for us to access not just Disneyland but also Paris itself; we caught the train down into the city centre from here and it was MILES cheaper and closer than any other campsite we could find anywhere near Paris (and there are simply NO camper stops anywhere near Paris City centre). No need to book (in fact I don't believe you can book), you just turn up early the morning (as the charge is per DAY, not per night- so as long as you leave before the park opens again the next day, you can just pay the €35). We were there in late May and there were probably 40 vans there. I guess in the summer it gets very busy but, that said, there was LOTS of space available. **N. 48,87500 E2,79700**

9. Barcelona, Spain: City centres can be a challenge to visit with a motorhome. Busy roads, one way systems, traffic and tight European streets can make it all seems like a bit too much effort. Not so if you can find the right camper stop, which we did in Barcelona. This place was a big, ugly car park, on the outskirts of the city, but it was manned 24/7 by a friendly security guard (who gave us a map and some excellent directions). There was a lovely clean shower block and family room, plus it was right next to the Metro station so it was easy as pie to get into (and out of Barcelona). It was a little expensive at €30 a night but it was a brilliantly convenient way to see this fabulous city that we wouldn't have missed for the world. **N41.42433 e2.20748**

10. Vessem, The Netherlands: This was another of those

lucky finds that just happen from time to time and mean that you end up staying in a place for three times as long as you had planned to! This camper stop, when we arrived, turned out to be a grassy parking area, situated just outside a campsite. For just €10 per night for 4 of us (plus a bit more for the third child) we could camp outside of the gates on the nice grassed area, but still make use of the fabulous campsite facilities. There were three huge outdoor swimming pools, one of which was a shallow, toddler- friendly one (perfect for a daughter with a plaster cast on her arm), FREE mini-golf, some giant inflatable pillows to bounce on, a terrific play area and a decent shower block. This is not what you should expect from most camper stops! This was deluxe!! **N51.41197 E5.27490**

TOP TEN FAMILY BEACHES:

1. Cabopino, Costa Del Sol, Spain: Having spent many childhood holidays here, I have an emotional connection to the place. However, there is no denying that this is one of the best beaches on the Costa Del Sol. Soft, silky sand, a great beach bar (plus a cute marina 2 mins walk away with some nice restaurants), shallow lagoon-like waters and a nature reserve just behind it. For me, it is close to heaven.

2. Lemvig beach, Denmark: See info in 'Ten best camper stops' above. Huge swathes of windswept, sandy dunes and gloriously windswept seas. Totally unspoilt. Well off the beaten track!

3. San Sebastian, Spain: For city beaches, this is hard to beat. The city itself is absolutely terrific and then, within spitting distance, you walk straight onto this lovely sandy bay, with beautiful calm waters and even some sea platforms to swim out and dive off into the deep, crystal waters. This main beach is called La Concha, then there's another beach which is great for families just a little further along the front and there's a surfers' beach too. I've also heard that there's another small island beach. So if you're looking for the beach and the city in one place (with the MOST amazing food scene- see Section 8 for more info) then San Sebastian is for you.

4. Montegordo, Portugal: You're spoilt for choice all along the Algarve. We could list several beaches that we loved in this region but our favourite was Montegordo at the calmer Eastern End of the Alarve. Perfect for anyone with accessibility issues, there are no dunes to mount to gain access to the sand. Long walkways connect the car park and the beach and the sand is fabulously soft and almost white. Great area for swimming (and warm enough for skinny dipping, even in the winter-according to my kids!).

5. Middlekerk, Belgium: This was actually not our first visit to the Belgian coast but we feel it is a massively underestimated holiday destination. It's so easy to get there from the UK (under an hour's drive from the Dunkirk ferry port) and the beaches are vast and glorious. All along the coast there are some lovely seaside towns, but Middlekerk was our favourite. This lively seafront is full of play areas and parks, there are places to hire all kinds of fun pedal powered contraptions (bicycle-car for ten anyone?). There are also oodles of great ice-cream, waffle and chocolate parlours. We noticed a few trendy beach bars too. There was even a pop-up cinema on the beach when we visited in the summer of 2017. Beautiful, soft sand and lovely shallow waters. Seriously- why not consider it for your next holiday?

6. Javea/Xàbia, Spain: This coastal resort in Alicante is a calm bay between two rocky outcrops and it's a popular tourist destination- we can see why. There are several great playgrounds on the beach for the kids to have fun in whilst you sample the deliciously cheap wine in the bars along the front before heading off to one of the charming family restaurants. The lovely long promenade is full of shops and there's plenty to amuse all ages here. I have a friend who moved to Javea from the UK and I am incredibly jealous!

7. Les Issambres, France: On the bay, near San Tropez. We stayed here on a day that was like something from the apocaplyse- the winds were so strong that I thought the van might flip over. However, in the morning when the rain passed we could see that this looked like an absolutely beautiful place to come for a summer holiday. There are 8 km of gorgeous inlets and sandy beaches. There were tons of extravagant campsites with waterparks etc and plenty of ice-cream shops! It is backed by a nature reserve and as we drove through it we saw scores and scores of wild flamingoes which was magical. We plan to return in the future (when the sun is shining).

8. Lake Balaton, Hungary: This one scores points for being so entirely unexpected. We were bombing it though Hungary in order to try to make it to Budapest but we were forced to stop somewhere for the night and I happened to look at the map and see that there was a big lake nearby. A slight detour would mean we could stay there overnight in a cheap camper stop (which turned out to be an extraordinarily old lady's back garden!). We walked down to the lake to see what it had to offer and we were absolutely ASTOUNDED by what we found. The kids were convinced that we were lying about it being a lake-"This is the sea Mum! There's no way this is a lake- we can't even see the other side!" They had a point. This is the largest lake in Central Europe and you feel like you're at the seaside but this is freshwater and you can swim in it, ski on it, boat on it, enjoy the beaches, the play areas and the cycle routes. I believe there is a big electronic music festival here ever summer. I'll bet it's a blast!

9. **Ardeche, France:** OK, this is another inland beach. It's on the banks of the Ardeche river, but we spent one of our finest beach days here. We set up our picnic on the sandy river bank, took the canoe out underneath the beautiful natural rocky bridge that the river has created and generally chilled out, building sandcastles and splashing about in this most beautiful place. And the brilliant thing about river beaches is that there are no crashing waves to beware of. There were even a couple of 'river police' officers out in their canoe, reminding us to wear life-jackets and keeping everyone safe. Great day. Beautiful memories!

10. Sagres, Portugal: This is the other end of the Algarve from Montegordo beach (see no. 4) and it could be a different world. Driving up to Sagres you feel like you are literally about to fall off the earth! Here, at the extreme Southwesterly point of Europe, the wind blows wind and the landscape is rugged, barren and lonely. But boy, is it jaw-droppingly dramatic and beautiful. There's a long and interesting historic past, linked to the exploration of the 'new world' but you won't find many museums here, it just has a chilled out surf vibe, a few cheery cafes and some GREAT beaches! (We happened across a deluxe 5* family resort called Martinhal just up the road from here, If we ever win the lottery we'll be coming back to stay there! **https://www.martinhal.com/sagres/en**)

TOP TEN CULTURAL DESTINATIONS WITH KIDS:

Europe is a vast treasure trove of culture and history. Almost everywhere you turn, you can learn or experience something new. I know that holidays are often a time when you just want to kick back and relax with your children, not always wanting to force them into 'learning'. However, for those times when you've got a little more patience, or for when you yearn to show your kids a bit more of the big wide world, here are the places we recommend for family culture:

1.Barcelona, Spain: Barcelona has SO much to offer. We chose to focus our attention on Gaudi whilst we were there, introducing our kids to this visionary artist whose legacy is so strong in Barcelona. You can show them Park Guell, which is lots of fun to run around, various other buildings around the city which bear Gaudi's striking designs and the fabulous Sagrada Familiar which is simply breath-taking. Honestly- even for kids. My older two couldn't get enough of this place. The natural forms that Gaudi took inspiration from and his use of vibrant colours make this unfinished cathedral so different from any other religious building you are likely to have seen. Barcelona also offers a great taste of Spanish culture- you can eat tapas in the bodegas, visit the Olympic park, walk around the Gothic old town and you MUST visit the food market at La Boqueria- an enjoyable assault on all your senses! Then, after soaking up all that culture, you can head to the beach for a well-earned rest!

2. Pompeii,Italy: I remember learning, at school, about how Mount Vesuvius erupted and buried the town of Pompei under its boiling hot lava, preserving much of it for centuries. I remember thinking that was sad, but not very interesting. Well, let me tell you, to see Pompeii in the flesh is absolutely incredible. It chills you to the bone to walk around this ENORMOUS city that was full of life one minute and wiped out the next. I had simply no idea of the scale of the tragedy until we visited. The reason this is a great place to visit with kids is that it is largely free of any kind of stuffy guides asking you to be quiet and not touch anything- you can run around and make as much noise as you like, whilst clambering over ancient stones, learning about the different types of baths and giggling at the rude drawings in the ancient 'lupanar' (brothel). Then you can rest for a while in the nice cafe before trooping off to learn how to stage your own gladiatorial battle in the amphitheatre and pretend to buy your dinner at the Thermopolium (ancient street-food stall). I really felt like history had come alive that day and we bought some great books there to help us further our understanding. (Be warned though- the nearby modern town is not such a nice place to spend any time!).

3. Santiago de Compostella, Galicia, Spain : A Unesco world heritage site, people journey on pilgrimages from far and wide to visit the Cathedral which claims to house the remains of Saint James. The pilgrims follow the camino from various countries across Europe, looking out for the symbol of the shell to show them the way (see https://www.caminoadventures.com for route details). We found it incredibly moving to sit in the square and watch all these people arriving at their special destination- as we watched them laugh, cry, embrace and take the weight off their weary feet, we had a lovely conversation with our kids about sacrifice and commitment and determination. The city itself has lots to offer- a fabulous food market, some beautiful cathedrals, a nice park, good restaurants and a choice of museums. We particularly enjoyed marvelling at spectacle of the swinging botafumerio. This is a huge censor (one of the largest in the world)- which swings on a system of pulleys across the ceiling of the cathedral, casting around the smell of the burning incense. Apparently its arc is 65 metres! It's really quite something to witness! Of course, the burning of incense is an important part of the liturgy but we are also led to believe that the reason this censor is so huge is because of the huge number of pilgrims who traditionally arrived here, unwashed and rather pongy!

4. Salzburg, Austria: Salzburg is a beautiful, compact city with a host of activities to offer families. Mozart was born and raised here and you can visit both his modest childhood home (which has some cool high-tech features allowing you to listen to and play with his music on computers) and his more extravagant residence from his later successful years which is now also a museum. There is a very hands on Science museum (Haus der Natur) which has a zone dedicated to the science of Mozart, alongside a cool aquarium and lots of other child-friendly areas (including an area where you can operate and ride in a hydrolic lift). You can take a boat cruise down the scenic river and there are some superb parks (where you can pretend to be Julie Andrews and the children from the Sound of Music as you dance around the fountains). There's a funicular up to a well-preserved castle and you can even take a very steep cable car up to the top of Maria's mountain (which was still covered in snow at Easter-time) and feel as though you are on top of the world. It is a compact yet bustling city. Then sampling a few of the traditional beers brewed by the monks will help you chill out after a busy day of seeing the sights!

5. Covodonga, Spain: A tiny town, nestled in the Picos de Europa mountains, Covodonga plays a vital part in Spanish history. The legends tells us that the great Spanish hero Don Pelayo was visited by a vision of the Virgin Mary here in Covodonga which gave him the strength and courage to fight back against the Moorish invasion and so being the Reconquista (the Spanish reclaiming their land). There is also a waterfall which promises to bring marriage within a year to all who drink from it. We found it to be a beautiful, extremely interesting and very special place. After you've toured the museum and the sites, lit a candle in the chapel and threatened to make your children drink from the fountain, you can drive up the insanely steep mountain side roads to the Picos De Europa National park and scale some of its peaks. It's a fabulous and very beautiful place.

6. Porto, Portugal: Porto has a lot to offer. Located on the banks of the river Douro, you can learn all about how its position helped it to develop the famous drink Port (and try some for 'educational reasons' in one of the Ferreira). The massive iron bridge running over the river was designed by Mr Eiffel's prodigy and you can see where his influences lie. We loved taking a ride in one of the iconographic trams which have been in operation here for over 100 years and the kids enjoyed looking out for all the buildings covered in 'azulejos' the beautiful hand-painted tiles which adorn so many buildings here.

We also visited the Igreja de Sao Francisco which is a church decorated in over 100kg of gold leaf- literally everywhere you look is golden- it's like being in King Midas' house! What came as a surprise to us was that underneath the church you can visit the ancient catacombs where hundreds of bodies lie interred (you have to walk across lots of graves to get around the place) and there are scores of skulls on display. It was a pretty educational (and a little scary) experience for our elder children but a good opportunity to talk about mortality and the historical arguments between the Catholics and the Protestants. Also- don't miss the custard tarts (pastel de nata) they are SO GOOD!

7. Berlin, Germany: In the early part of our trip the kids were forced to endure lots of religious buildings as they are so often the key visitor attractions in European cities. No so in Berlin. Here, they were treated a very different sort of history lesson and it really seemed to capture their imagination. In learning about the wall that separated East and West Germany we came to talk about all sorts of interesting issues. I love the way that the city has preserved the line of the wall, it is now marked out by colourful pipes that run along the sky line, indicating places that would have been impossible to cross during the time of the separation. Checkpoint Charlie is still a bit of an eerie memorial to those troubled times and the open air exhibition there is really quite moving. There is also a striking Holocaust memorial near the Brandenburg Gate where 2711 huge concrete slabs cover an entire block of the city. Brandenburg gate itself is pretty impressive and as a city, Berlin is lively and easy to navigate.

8. Rome, Italy: As cultural cities go, Rome is pretty hard to beat. Walking up to the Colosseum and then entering its amphitheatre is a feeling I don't think we'll ever forget. Its easy to talk about the Gladiators but to actually see that famous fighting space up close and personal is such an amazing experience. We found the audio guides here to be child friendly and really illuminating. The walk around the amazing ruins at the next-door Palatine Hill are a great way to learn whilst letting the kids blow off some steam at the same time. There is a definite lack of informative signposts here but you can just relax and soak up the ancient ambiance or pick up a guide book and learn a bit more as you wander. The view from the top is just wonderful. Another great place to visit which makes you feel absolutely inconsequential in the world is the Pantheon which is just so vast that you barely notice that this Roman temple (now converted into a church) which has stood here for almost 2000 years, houses the famous artist Raphael's remains. The architecture of the oculus and the drainage systems will simply blow your tiny minds! (AND, it's FREE to enter!) Go and throw a coin in the Trevi fountain afterwards and pray that life gives you the chance to return. Rome is just too good to visit only once.

9. The Vatican City: I guess this really should be listed as part of the Rome entry above but there is just SO much to see here that the Vatican City deserves an entry all of its own.

Standing in St Peter's square on a sunny day makes you feel like you're in the scene of a movie and if you join the long (but pretty fast moving) queue to go inside St Peter's Basilica, you won't be sorry. This enormous church (it is not-as many think- a cathedral), where Catholics believe St Peter's remains lie, is really spectacular. You can even take the lift and then climb the steps to the top of the cupola and view the lavishly decorated Basilica from the dome itself. You get some incredible views across the city from the top. If you are an art lover then you MUST also visit the Vatican Art Gallery which houses 70,000 works of art including the Sistine chapel. If you visit with children there is an excellent children's audio guide which leads them on a treasure hunt, searching out mummified remains, old masterpieces and guides their eyes to just a few key pieces rather than trying to make sense of it all. Our nine year old loved it. To see the Sistine chapel at its absolute best, I would recommend booking yourself onto an early morning tour. Before the museum opens to the public, you get escorted around the gallery as the sun rises and you get to stand in peace, looking up at Michelangelo's iconic ceiling fresco masterpiece- with just a handful of people (rather than the thousands who will squeeze in later in the day). Well worth setting the alarm clock for. Whatever time you decide to visit, booking is essential.

10. Ribe Viking Centre, Denmark: The idea of the Viking centre is that visitors step right back in time and enter a real, working Viking village. Volunteers come and live or holiday here, sleeping in the longhouses, feeding themselves using traditional methods and farming the land or creating buildings using the traditional techniques of the Vikings. If you're used to the Disney-fied 'living history' museums that we have in the UK, it can feel a bit strange to be largely ignored by these people in costume, who are simply getting on with their

Viking lives rather than interested in giving you a tour of the centre. However, once you get used to this vibe it is a truly remarkable experience to join in the role-plays by playing some viking games (throwing a massive caber-like-stick; balancing on a fallen tree whilst whacking each other with sacks; wrestling with a big rope!), visiting the market place, forging your own coin and grinding your own flour. Our children also took part in a Viking battle lesson (with armour, swords and shields), tried their hand at archery and stick-whittling then watched people make glass beads and carve the walls of the new church. We happily spent the whole day here and could easily have visited again a second day. The great play area and cafe sealed the deal for making this a truly wonderful family experience. (The little town of Ribe is also pretty great- see 'Top ten cheap or free Camper-stops' above).

TOP TEN CITIES TO VISIT WITH KIDS:

Before our trip I think I considered European city-beaks to be the bastion of the adult couple. The idea of taking my children off to see a city would have filled me with horror. But, reader, I was wrong! Kids have a brilliant time in cities and as long as you keep them well watered and fed, they can lead you to see some of the most beautiful places on our continent through newly opened eyes!

1. Dubrovnik, Croatia: When you first set eyes on the old Town in Dubrovnik, it leaves you speechless. It is simply the most spectacularly beautiful city. White limestone streets shimmer and shine almost as much as the beautiful Adriatic sea that surrounds it. The city is 'Game of Thrones' mad at the moment as it was the main filming location for King's Landing (with very little need for special effects). As you walk around it, you do feel like you're in another world. For culture, you can walk the old town walls which fortify and surround the city and/or take a boat trip over to one of the beautiful Elafiti islands and learn about the wildlife there. You can also ride the cable car up onto the top of Srd Hill for some amazing views (where you can visit the museum at the top devoted to Croatia's terrible civil war) and then chill out on the pebbly beach. It's easy to navigate Dubrovnik's streets and there are lots of family-friendly inviting cafes and restaurants just waiting to invite you in. One word of caution- don't expect it to be cheap. We found the rest of Croatia to be very affordable, but Dubrovnik's prices for drinks and meals etc. were akin to London prices. Dubrovnik is also a great base to take a day trip to Montenegro or Bosnia (sadly, we didn't have time for this but we plan to do that next time visit!).

2. Seville- We loved Seville SO much that it would be one of the first cities we would return to, given free choice. We spent two weekends there and still felt there was lots we hadn't seen. The Real Alcazar is a Unesco listed palace with both Christian and Moorish architecture combined to make this breathtaking spectacle of a building with all sorts of pools and patterns and tiles to admire. There are superb gardens with nooks and crannies to hide in all over the place. If you lose each other in here, you will be looking for a long time! It's absolutely stunning- even the kids thought so! Then just across the road from the Alcazar is the world's largest Gothic cathedral- another absolute spectacle. Then you've got the beautiful old town with its university and lively shopping areas, brilliant bars and restaurants, many of which have a bull-fighting flavour (Seville has one of the world's most famous bull-fighting arenas). The Plaza de Espana took us competely by surprise- it was barely mentioned in our guide book but it's a gorgeous place, a huge brick and tile extravaganza with mini canals and Venice-style bridges. You can hire a little row boat and merrily row your way around, gleefully spotting the frescoes depicting a variety of European locations. This is situated within the lovely park de Maria Luisa, where you can hire huge family-sized bicycle/car contraptions.

In fact, the whole city is really cycle-friendly; daily cycle use in the city has increased ten-fold since they built a network of safe, easily navigable cycle lanes. And you thought that was all? You still need to go and walk the skyline of the very modern, very controversial Metropol Parasol (known locally as Las Setas- the mushroom) and wander the beautiful old cobbled streets, under the orange trees, watching the live flamenco in the street and the hum of the beautiful Spanish guitar. As if you needed any more attractions, we were there at Christmas time and there was a fabulous Christmas market complete with big wheel and ice-skating rinks. There was also some sensational street-food. Being a university town, there's a big market for cheap, delicious food and drink. What a great place to visit- just writing this is making me want to book plane tickets right back again!

3. Budapest, Hungary: At the time we visited, George Ezra had recently released his single in which he laments "my heart's in Budapest, my hidden treasure chest." When we arrived we could see what he meant. Having driven through some fairly grey, deprived areas of eastern Europe we felt astonished to arrive into the grandeur of Budapest. Straddling the enormous Danube river, Budapest is, in fact, two cities- Buda on one side of the river and Pest on the other. It was a sunny day when we were there so we didn't feel the need to visit any of the numerous museums or splendid buildings (though I felt very tempted by the open air Memento Park- which Lonely Planet describes as a "socialist Disneyland" full of old Marxist statues and remains which have been rescued from rubbish heaps! Instead, we just wandered around enjoying the fabulous parks (there were lots), watching the world go by and enjoying the wonderful cheap food—if you visit you must try the kurtoskalacs (see Section 8 for more info) that the street vendors sell. A trip to Heroes' square made us feel very insignificant in the world. Being in Budapest felt a lot like being in London; the architecture is of a very similar era and scale, and the city has a similar kind of vastness with very distinct districts and areas to explore. The metro here is the oldest electrified underground system in the world (and it feels it!) but it's easy and cheap to navigate. It was strange to be so far away from London but to feel so much at home there. For our kids, a superb Lego exhibition was the icing on the cake- they loved this city!

4. Copenhagen, Denmark: If you follow any travel feeds on Instagram you will definitely have seen pictures of Nyhaven-

the colourful, beautifully restored old wooden houses which form the backdrop to this lovely old port in the centre of Copenhagen. There are tons of great bars and restaurants along the river here and to sit out in the Danish sunshine enjoying the world's best pastries and buns can only make you happy! Copenhagen is a great place to visit- it's small enough to walk or-even better-cycle around (although there are boat buses and trams too) and a place where families are made to feel very welcome. We found lots of wonderful open spaces and parks in this very green city (some even had ride on toys and bikes etc for the kids) and there were also some fantastic free swimming areas. The pools were too cold for us to enjoy in June (although there were some hardy Scandinavians enjoying an icy dip!) but I'll bet they are fabulous when the weather is warmer. The Scandinavians are brilliant at creating galleries and exhibitions which are child-friendly and Copenhagen has masses of these- it also has a pretty spectacular amusement park right in the city centre- Tivoli Gardens- founded in 1843 (apparently loved by both Hans Christian Anderson and Walt Disney). It has rides for both thrill seekers and nostalgia-lovers and hosts live music concerts on a regular basis. Ok, Copenhagen is going to set you back a few quid but it's really a wonderful place and, in our opinion, very much worth it.

5. Lisbon, Portugal: I never would have thought to visit Lisbon on a city break, it isn't one of those obvious choices like Rome or Barcelona is it? But I think this is an oversight-it's a wonderful city with so much to offer. As we emerged from the Metro we were pleased to find that the building is a piece of art in itself. It is covered in the famous azulejos (tiles) and you can't help but smile at the amazing level of detail involved. Each one has been hand-painted. This got us started on something of an azulejo treasure-hunt as everyone strained their eyes to look for the next example. Vasco da Gama set out from Lisbon in 1497 and was the first to reach India from Europe by sea. Being at the heart of global exploration helped to make Lisbon a very rich city indeed. Sadly though, in 1755 a massive earthquake destroyed most of the city. It was rebuilt in a rather hasty and efficient way- it now has a simple grid pattern with lots of wide streets and plazas which make it easy to navigate and enjoy. Alfama is one the oldest surviving districts and we enjoyed wandering this labyrinth of steep, narrow, cobbled streets which lead up to Lisbon castle. If you're lucky, like us, you'll hear some of the haunting Fado music whilst you wander in this traditionally poor area of the city. Fado was born here in Alfama; it is the musical expression of the Portuguese nation and it is their own version of the blues. Typically, the vocal drip with heartache. I really loved find out out that the Portuguese use music as a form of protest- a few years' ago, the opera singer Ana Maria Pinto led the crown in song to drown to the president's speech in a fightback against austerity! But don't leave yet- you must take a rustic tram down to the Belem district of the city, further along the waterfront. Here you will not only find the original source of the amazing pastel de nata (see Section 8 for more info) at the Pasteis de Belem but you'll be delighted by the beautiful park, historic moments, striking buildings (go and see the MAAT art gallery just for its architecture if nothing else) and the lovely laid back waterfront area near Belem Tower. It feels a bit like Covent Garden by the sea!

6. Venice, Italy: I had heard that Venice was expensive, overcrowded and a bit smelly. Not one to be discouraged, I still wanted to visit for myself and see the iconic city before it disappears forever into the water. Well, honestly, sitting on the water taxi and coasting into Venice, during 'Carnivale' was one of the highlights of my life and something I will never forget. Venice is, quite simply, amazing. Maybe it does get too busy and a bit smelly in the summer but I'll tell you what, in February at Carnival time it is pure magic. To see the gondoliers in their stripey jumpers taking their rich clients along the canals and under some of the 400 bridges that connect the 118 islands which make up this city, you feel as though you are on the set of a movie. As we journeyed further towards the centre of the city, the costumes of the people embarking became more and more flamboyant with every stop. Thousands of people were parading around in outfits that must have set them back hundreds of pounds and it all began to feel like a very weird and wonderful dream. Well, of course, we felt we had to join in- the kids and I bought some elaborate masques and had such a great day feeling part of this huge masquerade. I think to visit at carnival time has got to be the most special time you could visit, but at any time of year you are certain to enjoy amazing food (the pizza and gelato that we ate sitting out on the streets tasted better than anything I've ever eaten in the UK) and an incredible sense of drama and history. The tiny, twisted streets full of interesting merchants and the shops behind the Piazza San Marco are a great way to while away an afternoon- you can watch the cooks and the craftsmen hard at work though their windows and marvel at the detailed cakes and costumes they are creating before your eyes. St Mark's Basilica is stunning and supposedly houses the remains of Saint Mark (so that was three of the four evangelists' graves we had visited by this point on our trip). It is also free to enter. So it's true- it isn't cheap to stay in Venice or eat and drink in the cafes, BUT the street food is very affordable, in plentiful supply and totally delicious. Yes- the transport is expensive- I believe an hour on a gondola costs about €120 but you can take the boat taxi for a fraction of the cost and see the same things. You can also walk around most of the city- even with kids. It's a bit of a labyrinth but what better place to get lost? We had only planned to visit for one day but we had so much fun that we returned for a second day and had the most spectacular time here. Definitely one for your bucket-list.

7. Paris, France: Not just a city for a romantic couple we discovered; kids will love a visit Paris. Ours were enormously excited to visit the Eiffel Tower, having seen it in so many books. By this point in the trip we had run out of money so we didn't bother going up it (€19 each to take the stairs, €25 to take the lift), but they were perfectly happy to have a picnic on the grassy banks opposite and play at sliding around on the marble steps! We wandered down the Seine (singing "walks along the Seine" from 'Mama Mia'), crossed the fun footbridges, shopped at the antique stalls along the banks of the river and were wowed by the beautiful buildings. We whiled away an hour or two in the lovely park- Jardin de Tuileries- next to the Louvre (ice creams helped) and then ambled up to see Notre Dame which is just beautiful. The charming cobbled streets and chances to try crepes, croissants, moules and croque-monseiur kept us all happy and the sunshine made it an easy day. By night, the Sacre Coeur will capture your hearts and you can soak up the ambience of the street musicians as you wander around Monmartre. Paris doesn't need to dent your wallet too much. Then there's Disneyland; Disneyland *will* dent your wallet. Let's be honest-it will smash a huge hole in it. But you might just find the magic is to much to resist! (Plus you can get some good bargains if you book online, in advance, avoid the school holidays, take your own packed lunches, drinks and snacks, avoid the gift shops and if you camp overnight in the carpark (see the section above on 'Best Camper stops').

8. Barcelona- See 'Top Ten cultural places to visit'-above. You will love Barcelona for its Gaudi, tapas and pintxos, wine, the Bari Gothic (Old Town), the beach, the superb art galleries. ... oh- and I almost forgot- the football club FCB is amazing and the tour is great. If you've got football fans in your family don't miss it! Take note- Barcelona is a huge and sprawling city- the open-top bus tour can be a great way to save little ones' legs whilst still seeing most of the landmarks. There are three main routes which will get you around all of the major sites. The main problem is deciding which stops to get off at!

9. Berlin- For engaging modern history, a vibrant city, the

Lego Discovery Centre, great shopping and multi-cultural cuisine (see 'Top Ten cultural places to visit' above).

10. Rome- For mind-blowing Roman history, amazing monuments, sensational gelato, pizza, pasta, music and wine, and the romantic ambience, (see 'Top Ten cultural places to visit' above).

PRACTICAL TIPS FOR FAMILY TRAVELLERS

So, you're thinking of emulating our adventure and going off on your own big trip? Good for you! Here are some of our more practical tips to help you avoid some of the pitfalls we fell into. Keep the faith and don't give up- it'll be one of the best things you ever do.

BUYING A CAMPER VAN (FOR NOVICES);

We are, by no means, experts in this area. You can find lots of guidance online and in great books like 'Go Motorhoming and Caravanning' (Vicarious Media). We used this book as our bible and took it with us when viewing vehicles. In the end, we were under pressure to buy something quickly and fell into a bit of a trap because we knew we were going to be homeless and the right van just wasn't turning up on the secondhand market. We ended up impulse-buying from a dealer because we needed the security of knowing we had somewhere to live! There was a van which had only done 7,000 miles and had been used as a 'show' van by the dealership so it had lots of mod cons and we avoided the huge taxes involved in buying a brand new vehicle. We were also advised that motorhomes generally hold their value and that we could sell it on our return, recouping most of our money. The dealership insisted they would be first in line to buy it back.

Well, in some ways our van was a good purchase and in other ways we felt we'd made a mistake. It was superb not to have to worry too much about the breakdown-factor of an older van. Given that our van was so new and shiny, we didn't experience any mechanical issues in our 20,000 mile trip which was amazing. Other travellers we met, who were driving older vans, were held up on a few occasions by inevitable break-downs and failings. A new van obviously also comes with a degree of comfort from its modern trimmings and gizmos and all of this was great. However, it was painful to experience the gradual breaking and tarnishing of the van as the year wore on. These vehicles are not built for living in, so as the knobs fell off the cupboard doors and the trim came away in places and the floor wore thin and dirty, we couldn't help but feel that our money was burning away in from of our eyes! On our return our not-so-friendly-dealer wanted nothing to do with buying our van back from us as he had all his 2017 models to sell (clearly, these people will say anything to make a sale).

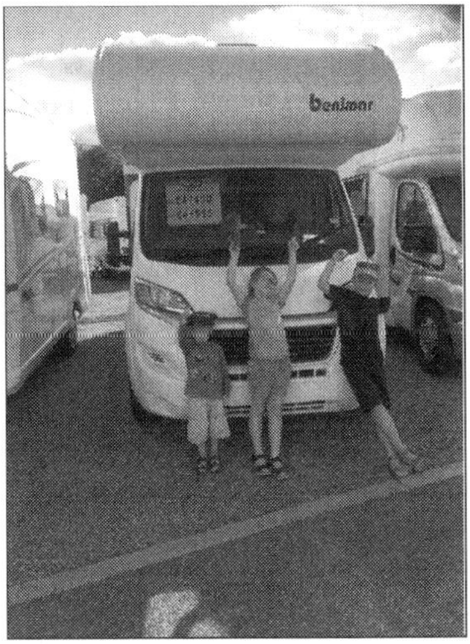

It would also be true to say that we fell in love with the van on our journey and we did spend a lot of time thinking that we would keep 'Beni' and maintain a sense of adventure in our lives once we got home. We planned to get away for a night or two every other week. Needless to say, in six months of being back, we haven't managed to do this even once- modern life is just too busy. So we are now saddled with a rather expensive asset which we pay reasonably large amounts of money to tax, insure and store whilst we get the broken bits repaired. We do plan to sell it very soon, but resale value is something you should research carefully before you sign on the dotted line.

The main things you need to bear in mind when looking for a Motorhome are:

- **Number of seatbelts**- it is *extremely* difficult to get an extra seatbelt added to a purpose-built motorhome. If, like us, you need that 5th seatbelt, this will rule out A LOT of vans.

- **Number of berths-** some vans require you to turn seating areas into beds. Will you cope with doing this every night? It is a big faff. We opted for fixed bunk beds instead and would highly recommend it. Even if it means you have less living space, it does mean everyone has a (small) space of their own to retreat to in times of need.
- **Weight-** check your licence. If you passed your driving test since 1st Jan 1997, you will only be able to drive a van with a MAM up to 3,500kg. This will massively reduce the number of vans you can consider. As more and more younger drivers take up motorhoming, the manufacturers will start to adapt to this weight limit, but at present, the majority of motorhomers still took their test long before 1997 and so most motorhomes weigh over 3,500kg. You can have the MAM of a vehicle adjusted but it will take time and money so its not an option if you're in a hurry.
- **Left hand Drive?** We really wanted a left-hand drive vehicle. It would have made life easier for us but they simply don't come onto the UK market that often. You can import from Europe but, again, this will take time, paperwork and money. In reality, I'd say it really wasn't too bad driving on the right in a right-hand-drive vehicle. You soon get used to it. If you've got someone in the passenger seat at all times, it really isn't much of an issue- they can look left and operate all the tolls for you!
- **Water ingress:** I'd say if there's one thing to be super-wary of when you view a motorhome, look for signs of water coming in. This is like the cancer of motorhomes. We were very keen to buy one we saw on

private sale but when I lifted the mattress on the over-cab bed, there were lots of blue mould patches where water had clearly sat for a while. My understanding is that over-cab beds can be a particular place where leaks can happen so do look carefully and ask questions about this.

Various other factors were influential in making our decision:

- cost
- an oven
- a large garage area for storage
- good sat nav system
- decent radio
- dining table all 5 of us could sit at comfortably
- roll out side-awning bar (so useful)
- external bbq point
- gas system (we favour refillable LPG fixed tank).
- length (for storage, parking and ferry prices, shorter is better)
- height
- levels of insulation (if you are only doing sunny breaks, a van-conversion might be the right van for you, but you're doing any winter-travelling, you will really need something which is better insulated and equipped with proper heaters).

There's a great checklist of questions to ask in Vicarious Media's 'Go Motorhoming and Campervanning' book.

I think in many ways buying a campervan is like buying a house. You can research and read so much, you can ask a mechanic to check it over, you can get a habitation check done to make sure it's safe but it will always be a bit of a step into the dark. There's no point holding out for the 'perfect' van because it probably doesn't exist. We live in hope that what we were told is true- they should generally hold their value pretty well, so if you make the wrong decision you should be able to resell it and buy another one. Most long-termers we spoke to were on their second or third van.

GETTING STARTED IN YOUR MOTORHOME:

If you are anything like us, you will drive away from the motorhome handover realising that you can remember NOTHING you were just told! Our hearts filled with dread as we realised that we hadn't listened carefully enough about how to empty the toilet or the water tanks or use the leisure battery or anything! Fear not. You WILL work it out and if you can't, there will almost always be a helpful fellow English-speaking camper to offer advice and show you the ropes. There is always the internet too- god bless the internet- which will answer most of your questions in a heartbeat. However, for true novices who are lost and alone here are the most basic things you need to know:

The toilet: Most UK campers use a product largely referred to as 'toilet blue'. You need to pour a capful of it into the bottom of the toilet cassette, along with a couple of capfuls of water. This toxic blend of chemicals will ensure that any deposits you make in the loo will not stink you out and will dissolve in there until you find a proper place to dispose of them. Emptying the toilet was always my husband's job. His top tips are to buy the cheapest loo paper (as it will dissolve more easily) and to try not to poo into it too soon before emptying it as the chemicals won't have a chance to dissolve the solids; they will rattle around the cassette and be hard to evacuate. You may even be forced into some grim poking-around-with-a-stick antics! You are advised to do your best to poop in public/campsite/restaurant toilets as often as possible! Making up a spray bottle of dilute blue which you can spray around the toilet bowl after use will also make your lives less smelly. NB. I am very aware that this blue stuff is not at all good for the environment. On the one hand, you can consider how much water you save from all the flushing you aren't doing, on the other hand, your toxic waste does need to go somewhere after a couple days in the van. We were put to shame by our Brave-Brighton friends who were using a plastic box full of soil in place of their toilet cassette and then burying their 'dirty deeds' every day. However, the stories they told of how bad the smell was and how challenging it could be to find a place to bury the poop did make us feel we weren't up to the job (so to speak). There is a 'green' product available and I plan to try this next time we venture out. It certainly wasn't widely available across Europe. In truth, during the whole year, we probably only got through four or five bottles of blue so the impact we had was pretty minimal.

Batteries: Your van will have a leisure battery as well as the normal vehicle battery. The leisure battery charges as you drive and there should be an indicator inside the van which shows you how much charge it has got at any one time. Any electrical items inside the van will run off the leisure battery if you are parked up and not plugged into electric hook-up. We found that the longest we could go without getting panicky was about three days (and we'd have to be quite careful about usage- not charging too many things, watching the TV or using the lights for too long). If we were off grid for just a day it was fine to blast away on the TV and heating-which are the biggest consumers of charge. It was nice to know we could always get warm! If it ran low and we weren't going to be on a campsite, we just needed to go for a drive and charge it back up again.

Gas: Our van came equipped with one full tank of Calor gas and space for a second one. The idea with the Calor gas tanks is that you use up the whole thing then purchase a new full one (trading in the old bottle). Having done some reading, we decided to upgrade by converting it to a fixed LPG tank which his refillable, cheaper to fill and much more versatile. You can fill up the tanks at petrol stations, in much the same way as filling up with Petrol or diesel. We were aware that LPG is not widely available in Spain and Portugal and that some places would be funny about us filling up a tank, but in truth we didn't run into many problems. I think twice (across the year) the petrol station assistant wouldn't let us fill up because it was going into a small tank and in Spain although LPG wasn't available everywhere, we used a brilliant app called **www.mylpg.eu** which helped us to locate the nearest fuel station which did have it. We had two tanks installed and we found that this kept us going for absolutely ages. The installation was expensive, in the region of £750 but the savings and ease of use more than made up for it. Filling up with LPG is MUCH cheaper than replacing Calor gas cannisters. It would typically cost us about €5-6 every couple of weeks. We never managed to run out of the stuff and I'd say that two full tanks, on a similar rate of usage to ours would last you, on average, three weeks. The LPG fuels the stove, oven, fridge and the heating (when you are not hooked up to electricity) and there are dials on the top of the bottles so you can keep an eye on how you're doing. The fridge can be quite thirsty on gas when you're not on electric hook-up so just be aware of this and plan accordingly. If you are travelling extensively across Europe, I'd really recommend looking into getting your van converted to a fixed refillable LPG system.

NB: You must ALWAYS turn the gas off when you are driving-for safety. We put a note on the dashboard to remind us. Don't worry about the fridge- it will be powered by the charging leisure battery whilst you drive.

Water: You will need a 'food grade' hose to fill up your tank, plus a watering can would be useful for filling up from taps in tricky situations. We didn't have one as we simply didn't have enough space but there were times when a watering can would have come in useful! Make sure you are filling from a source which is drinking water 'potable' (France and Spain), potabile (Italy), Pitka soda (Croatia), drinkwater (Dutch), Trinkwasser (German). We would usually last about four days on a full tank, depending very much on whether we were on campsite or not. When on a campsite, we would wash up and use the showers in the facilities provided so we got through a LOT less water in the van. Vicarious Media say they use 20 litres per day (for two people) when parked off site and a tank will usually hold about 100 litres. We used our shower VERY infrequently, simply because it took ages to heat the water (and then you only had hot water for brushing your teeth etc), and even then the shower only lasted long enough for one of us. We tended to just boil a pan of water on the stove then put this in the bathroom sink and have a flannel wash with it. But then we were stopping at campsites every few days so we always knew there was a shower in sight!

There should be a gauge inside your van to let you know how much water you have in both the clean tank and the grey water tank (the water that goes down the sinks and shower drain). You will want to dump the grey water as often as possible. We found this really easy- lots of European petrol stations even have a water dumping area but if you're in the wilds you can simply find a drain that's easy to park over (you just park over the drain and pull the valve). This is fairly non-offensive water just from washing up and brushing your teeth etc. MAKE SURE YOU ALWAYS LET IT DRAIN COMPLETELY, otherwise yucky smells build up.

NB Water is heavy- (1 litre weighs 1kg) you will often not *need* to fill right up. Think ahead- if you're heading for a campsite, just leave yourselves enough in the tank to make a cup of tea along the way and consider driving with a much lighter tank- this is important to think about if, like us, you are restricted on the weight limit. It is also just a good idea, in general to keep yourselves light when possible-it will improve your fuel performance and improve your stopping distance.

Electricity: You will need to buy a long electric hook-up cable. Ours had three pins at the point where it met the van. Connecting to the hook up point across Europe can be a slight head-scratcher. We had a set of three different adapters which allowed us to hook up to all of the different European plugs that we found- do not head off into Europe without buying these- we didn't find too many camping shops which stocked them! The voltage will change, depending on where you are and at times this means you have less of a supply coming in, so can't, for instance, power the microwave or plug in a hair dryer, but your fridge and lights will work fine. Once or twice we tripped the supply in a campsite by being too demanding (you might need to unplug the TV before you try to use the microwave etc) which does tend to make campsite owners a little grumpy! If you've bought a UK van, you will have English, three pin pug sockets inside your van. No need to bring European two-pin adaptors!

PAY LOAD:

This was an issue which caused us ENORMOUS amounts of stress before we left and absolutely no stress whilst on the road. If, like us, you passed your driving test after January 1st 1997, then you can only drive a vehicle up to 3,500kg. This will mean that unless you take an additional driving test (which seemed impossibly complex and difficult when we looked into it- you might be able to fathom your way through it- but we couldn't!), there will be many, many motorhomes on the market that you won't be able to legally drive. Once you've purchased a motorhome of the right weight, you have to make sure that you don't overload it. We read, with fear, that there would be road-side weigh-ins and weight checks at ferry ports. Our van, unladen, weighed 3,000kg, so that gave us 500kg to play with- this is called your 'payload'. As we tried to work out how we could possibly stay under 3,500kg MAM (Maximum Authorised Mass), we stood outside our house, weighing ourselves and every single item we loaded into the van, frantically tapping into the calculator and then arguing, at length, about what constituted an 'essential' item. Remember that a full tank of water will be about 100kg and a full tank of fuel approximately 90kg. Eventually, we gave up. 3,500kg might be enough if you're just off for a short break, but if you're heading off for a year, through the winter, you will need to find an alternative solution. (Remember- your payload has to include the weight of your family too so if you have less children and love handles than us you may find this a little easier!) We discovered that, in addition to the weight of your vehicle you can also tow a trailer (maximum weight 750 kg) so we had a tow bar fitted to the van (supplied by the brilliant guys at PWS in Dorset) at a cost of almost £2,000 and bought a trailer (another £750). What this meant was that we could legally now take along all of the things we wanted on our big adventure- like our massive side-awning (tent), our inflatable canoe, the life jackets, the walking boots etc, all of which made our trip much more enjoyable and manageable. It also allowed us to load up with lovely French wine before heading home to ease the pain of our trip ending! However, the trailer was also a massive pain in terms of driving, parking, getting ferries etc. Think carefully before getting one and only go for it if you REALLY need it. The number of times we kicked it in anger, before unhooking it and pushing it along (because it was almost impossible to reverse with the bl**dy thing on!) are too numerous to mention!

Needless to say, we saw no sign of any van ever being weighed by the police or to get on the ferry or at any other point. That's not to say it never happens, but we drove for a year and didn't see it ever.... (However, putting the chances of being caught-out to one side, if you were involved in an accident and were found to be driving an overweight vehicle, I do think you might run into problems with both your insurance company and the law so it's got to be best to try and keep to your limit).

SECURITY:

I don't know if we were just lucky or we made sensible choices or whether our motorhome- as it was a pretty new model-was fairly secure, but we didn't experience any security issues on our trip. Before we left, I had read, with fear in my heart, about motorhomes being targets for thieves and villains. My advice is to never stay in motorway service areas, if an area seems dodgy to you or there are suspicious people loitering, just move on and keep your most valuable belongings on you (or at least hidden from view). People we met were using steering locks and had fitted super-duper locks or alarms to their habitation doors or even trackers fitted to their vans. We felt pretty naive for not having done so- I mean you'd be pretty stuck if someone pinched your van (considering it's your home and contains all your worldly goods)- but anyway, we lived to tell the tale!

HOW TO NOT OVERCOMPLICATE YOUR LIFE- KEEP A UK POSTAL ADDRESS:

Modern life isn't too happy about letting you up-sticks and abandon everything. Some things get really complicated. If you intend to return to the UK, its pretty important to keep a UK postal address so that you can keep a bank account, stay on the electoral register and not have to actually 'live' abroad for the time you are away. Some very good friends let us use their address as our postal address whilst we were abroad. This meant that we were officially 'living' in the UK and just 'travelling' elsewhere. We could still vote, we could stay registered with a UK doctors (which helped with our EHIC and reassured us that we could get help fast in an emergency), and now that we are back, living in society again, we don't have to answer tricky questions about living abroad. It also meant we were able to apply for a mortgage and provide the previous 5 years' addresses without too much bother. I think most lenders won't lend to you if you've lived abroad in the past six months. Having a UK address also allowed us to tax and register our vehicles. I am not sure you can cope without a kind friend or family member who will allow you to do this. I was worried that we might negatively impact on her council tax or credit rating or something, but this was not the case at all; a person's credit rating is only affected by someone they share financial activity with (like taking out a loan or a mortgage or a bank account together). Apart from receiving bag-loads of junk mail and our few bits of useful post, I don't think it had a negative impact on our friends in any way.

PLANNING:

As I have mentioned before, I really would advise against doing too much planning before you hit the road. So much will change and develop as you go that much of your planning will be time wasted, However, that said, there are bound to be certain things that you don't want to miss and we found that the best thing to do was have a quick skim read of the guide book before entering a new country. Then I would sketch out a quick hand drawn map of the country and try to label its various regions. Then we would, together, plot onto this map the things that we'd heard or read about that we definitely wanted to see and do. This would then form the basis of our route and our planning. We would try to marry this up with some nice looking campsites and camper stops. We then had a lovely, one page, quick-to-view idea of where were and where we were going. It's very hard to get an overview and an understanding of the geography of an area from the road maps because the scale is just unmanageable for an overview. And if you don't know that names or geography of the various regions within a country, you can't make a great deal of sense of the guide book! Here is an example of my planning notes for Germany:

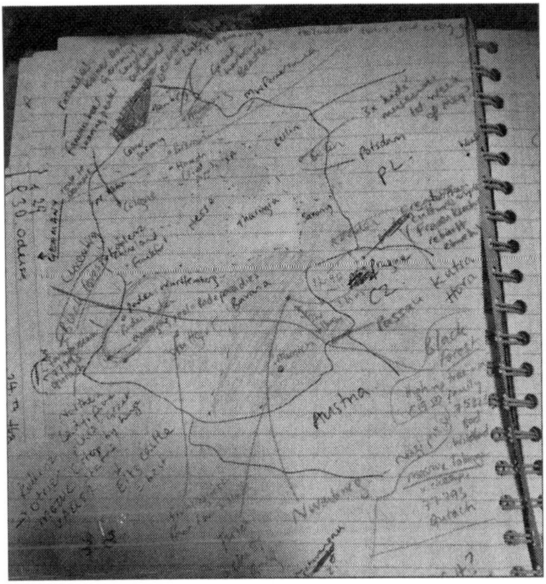

WHAT IS A CAMPER STOP OR AN AIRE? HOW DO THEY WORK?

In many European countries, motorhome stopover areas are provided, often with the intention of bringing tourists into little known areas and towns. Many of them are free, some have a small charge and they will usually have services you can utilise to fill up with water, dump your grey water and dump your toilet cassette. I think €6-€12 would be an honest average of what we paid to stay. They are often coin-operated so keep a stash of coins in the cab. In France and Belgium they are usually called Aires de Service or Stationnement Camping Car. In Germany, Austria and Switzerland they are known as Wohnmobil-Stellplatze. In Italy they are Aree di Sosta, In Norway- Bobil and in Spain and Portugal they are Area de Service para autocaravanas.

Motorhomes are an interesting area of the law because they are technically vehicles, which means the police have to allow you to stop and rest. It isn't officially 'camping' to sleep in one. This means that only motorhomes can stay in such Aires, not caravans, because Aires do not have licenses for 'camping'. For a similar reason, when staying in an Aire you are not allowed to get your awning, table and chairs, mats and toys etc all out and effectively set up 'camp' here. It is just supposed to be a parking area (which you are permitted use overnight). You *will* see people setting up camp occasionally, and from time to time, where it was clearly established practice and there were no local residents to disturb, we did get our table and chairs out or let the kids play out on the mat but it generally seen to be bad form and the motorhoming community fears that these fabulous facilities could be at risk of being shut down if people disregard the rules. Sometimes, there will be electrical hook up available for a small fee in an Aire but more usually you should expect to be off grid for the night. At first, I found the idea of an Aire a little daunting. We seem so vulnerable in a car park, open to anyone who wished to enter, but we got braver and more confident as the trip developed and these really were essential to us in keeping our costs down. We usually found we could stay a couple of nights in Aires before we needed to find showers and washing machines etc again, but if we were able to find an appropriate place to empty our toilet and fill up with water, towards the end of the trip it wasn't unusual for us to spend a whole week in camper stops. Many aires have a limit of one or two nights per vehicle so they are supposed to just be a temporary measure but that suited us and our nomadic lifestyle just fine! We found the book 'Camper stop Europe' which lists hundreds of places to stay for free or very cheaply (in a motorhome) by A.E.M. van den Dobbelsteen to be absolutely invaluable. We also regularly used an app called 'Park for the Night' which has user tips and reviews. It recommends both free-camping spots and cheap camper stops.

Lots of camper stops are municipally run but there are also plenty of privately run ones to be found (prices here can be much higher). You also find that some supermarkets will allow you to stay overnight and there are also plenty of restaurants who will allow you to stay for free if you buy a meal there. These won't always be listed in the books. Sometimes you just drive past and see a restaurant with a camper van on its sign. We found a super example of one such restaurant near Plitvicke Lakes in Croatia. After a wonderful but hard day's walking, we had been panning to stay in the nearby campsite but it was expensive and we were running low on food. Instead, we saw the camper stop sign at the local pizzeria and decided that we could spend the same money as it would cost to camp at the campsite, and we could have a slap up meal and a night in the huge car park of the pizzeria. They even let us use their bathrooms-it was perfect! The key to successful camper stopping is to not be too rigid or hopeful in your outlook and to always be open to the possibility of adapting your plans.

There are also lots of vineyards around Europe where you can stay for free as long as you buy a bottle of wine (or two). We actually didn't go for this option too often, but if we ever travel again without the kids- we will make a real road trip of this! There are several guide books you can buy which will direct you around Europe's vineyard camper stops.

WILD CAMPING/FREE-CAMPING/OFFSITE-PARKING:

Call it what you will, if you plan to stay for free, in areas other than designated motorhome stops, here is our advice: Scandinavia is your friend. In Finland, Iceland, Norway and Sweden the 'right to roam' means that any can camp almost anywhere as long as you are more than 150m from any houses, you only stay 2 nights maximum and you don't start fires or leave rubbish etc. We didn't make it too far into Scandinavia so we didn't experience these freedoms ourselves but we have friends who did and they said it was very much an accepted part of the culture. Anywhere near the Mediterranean and you will find it is a different story. In busy parts of the Med you will be moved on by the police (or worse) but it does depend very much on the season and how conspicuous you are. If you spend most of your time away from the van and don't cause anyone any problems you'll often find that you're left alone. We wild-camped probably fifty times and we were only moved on once (and that was at about 8am by a very friendly warden). The best thing to do is seek advice from others, use the 'Park for the night' app to see what other travellers have experienced and if in doubt, move away from the masses, move further inland and don't cause a nuisance to anyone. Finding a place where there is no definite sense of ownership like a municipal car park, leisure centre or a cemetery car park can be a good idea (although you do sometimes find that these are the places the youths choose to hang around at night revving up their scooter engines and racing around in the dark... don't say we didn't warn you!). It's probably best not to have an alcoholic drink that night just in case you have to move on.

Wifi and internet access: We hoped to escape too much internet fuss and just enjoy each other's company for a year. We were a little naive and underprepared for just how far wifi is ingrained into our lives now. I had taken out a fairly expensive mobile phone contract which gave me 4GB of roaming data per month. It certainly wasn't enough. We thought it would be OK to simply use wifi in cafes and campsites. Yes- lots of places do have it but we found that most campsites will charge you through the nose for it (and it is often extremely slow) and cafes tend to have slow speed or sporadic signal. In Portugal we were able to buy local SIM cards which gave us a lot of (or in one case -unlimited data) for a pretty small fee. It cost us about €10 per month. We could use this SIM card in a little portable wifi router which allowed us to connect several devices at once and it was great -while it lasted. They only worked in Portugal. We foolishly believed that we would find the same situation in the other countries we visited. This was, sadly, not the case. Similar products, in Spain, were about three times the price and the costs got higher the further into Europe we went! Toward the end of our trip, there was a change to UK law and I think UK mobile phone companies have now really dropped the price of data roaming within the EU but it is definitely something to try and get sorted before you leave the UK. Once you're abroad it becomes quite a challenge. It was clear to us that other campers had been able to set up their own mobile wifi (or mifi) with roof mounted antennae etc (we could see it when we tried to connect on campsites) but I'm afraid this was beyond our level of expertise! If we ever go off again, I will be sure to consult **www.motorhomewifi.com** to see what the best solution is!

PRACTICAL TIT-BIT TIPS:

- you can get most European **Lonely Planet** guides as part of the **Kindle Unlimited** package which is approximately £8 per month. This was great for us as we visited 19 different countries and didn't have space, weight allowance, or budget for 19 differerent guide books! I love the Lonely Planet series- I find the historical background sections really well researched and interesting plus I love the way they cater for travellers on a budget in terms of their restaurant (and other) recommendations.

- **Travel insurance** is easy to secure if you have no short return journeys to the UK planned during your travelling time. The fact that we needed to come home for two weddings made finding travel insurance quite challenging (though not impossible) see 'Section 5: Health Tips' for more info).If you can, go away and stay away until you're ready to come back for good. It makes life easier! Be aware that if an emergency does call you home, your travel insurance may become invalidated.
- **ACSI Camping card:** Having an ACSI camping card is a great idea. It gets you a discounted rate at over 3,300 campsites across Europe. When you visit one of these campsites, OFF-SEASON (and that's the key to ACSI success- you only get these discounts outside of the peak seasons), you can get a rate of either € 11, € 13, € 15, € 17 or € 19 a night. These are the only pricing options. This is for two people and includes your awning, electric hook up and hot showers. Some campsites will also include up to two kids for free, others will charge for the kids. This was our only grumble, it is often hard to find out, in advance, how much a campsite will charge for children. So we might arrive somewhere expecting the ACSI overnight rate of €17 but then be stung

with another €7 each for the three kids which really bumped up our costs! Other times we'd arrive and they would insist that the children were free, in which case we'd got an absolute bargain. We just learned to take the rough with the smooth! The other good thing about ACSI is that they inspect the campsites each year and provide non-biased reviews of each one; using your guide book and/or app you can find out all the information about the kinds of services provided at each site and you can see reviews written by other campers. You can even download different sections of Europe in the App so that you can use it offline and hunt for campsites even when you have no wifi signal. Membership of ACSI saved us, across the year, an enormous amount of money and we have continued our subscription as we found it to be such a good resource. It's only €15 per year. It's a no-brainer! More info at : https://www.campingcard.co.uk

- Be aware of local customs and habits. For instance, in many parts of Spain you can't even get a menu for dinner until 20:30pm, but when we were looking for dinner in the Netherlands, the fish and chip shop takeaway and restaurant closed for business at 7pm! Also, in Spain and Portugal we would frequently find ourselves turning up to a town in the mid-afternoon, only to find that everything was shut for the siesta period. Bank holidays frequently caught us out- it is worth going on Twitter and typing the name of the region you are visiting into the search bar. You should soon find out if there are any major events going on. And lastly, remember that, unlike the UK, in many parts of Europe everything closes on a Sunday. No-one wants to buy their dinner supplies from a petrol station!

- Remember that your trip isn't about proving anything to anyone else. Keep your goals and ideals in mind as you weather the storms and triumphs of each day. We were slightly sad to find that once we were home, after the initial set of standard questions, no-one really had any probing questions about our big adventure. It was almost as though it was too big a topic to cover in any one sitting. People soon got back to discussing the weather and all the other things they had been talking about before we left! Whilst our year abroad might well give us useful anecdotes for years to come, it isn't going to make us instantly interesting to everyone else. And that's ok.
- Don't expect every minute of every day to be golden sunshine and smiles. You *will* get on each others' nerves, you *will* miss your creature comforts and you *will* get bored of route planning. I remember having a sudden realisation that route planning and finding campsites etc had become our new 'daily grind', the new boring, mundane routine! I guess everything in life can become that way. Then the next day we visited the Lindt factory and I stood looking at photos of cocoa farmers in Cote D'Ivoire which gave me a bit of a reality check about how bloomin' lucky I am.

Things you will need but you don't realise it yet:

- **Lightweight travel towels:** drying things in a camper van is one of the major pitfalls of living in one. There is so little space. The lightweight, specialist travel towels are so quick to dry and many of them have anti-microbial properties. You will avoid the perilous situation of having wet, heavy, smelly towels hanging around all day. AN ABSOLUTE MUST.

- **Fluffy crocs:** I used to mock people who wore plastic croc-style shoes in public. I never will again. Crocs are the PERFECT camping shoes. You will want to keep your van as clean and mud free as possible, so will need to keep taking your shoes on and off a million times day. I thought flip flops would suffice but I soon discovered that walking through wet or dewy grass first thing in the morning, en route to the toilet block, made for cold toes and a sad start to the day! Wearing crocs with fluffy lining means you feel like you've got your slippers on but you can still manage to do wet or dirty jobs like empty the toilet cassette, fill up with water or visit some questionable bathrooms! You can pick them up for a couple of Euros in Spanish pound-type-shops.
- **Podcasts:** We love music on a long drive but we did SO much driving that we ran out of songs that we wanted to listen to anymore (and there's only so much Europop radio one can take). Finding some interesting podcasts meant that long journeys became about more than just getting somewhere, we were learning something along the way. Some of our favourites were: History on Fire, This American Life, Woman's Hour, Desert Island Discs, The Drunken Taoist and the Duncan Trussell Family hour. And for kids: Stories podcast, Brains On, Wow in the World and Tumble.
- **Onboard tv/DVD player with 12volt adaptor:** Yes, we did want to get away from TV and

spend our lives outdoors or reading but we have three kids and we live in the real world. And we did A LOT of driving. And sometimes it rained. So we were extremely grateful to have purchased, at the last minute, a little TV with integrated DVD player to mount on the wall above the habitation door which all three kids could watch from the comforts of their seats whist we drove along. They were so much happier on long journeys when they were entertained by the genius of Toy Story/Home Alone/Disney movies etc. And what I particularly liked was the way in which they would also watch the special features (desperate for something new to watch). There's a lot of good stuff in those special features! For instance, on Toy Story 3 there's loads of great information about how the film was made and how people can become animators. These were often really educational for the kids. Having a 12 Volt adapter (cost approx £12) means you can use an electronic device when not hooked up to an electrical supply. So we needed this to make the TV work (off the leisure battery) whilst we were driving along. Best money ever spent!

- **Surface wipes:** You can't always access the taps very easily (the sink is also the chopping board) so those antibacterial surface wipes are a life savers, not just for wiping the van counters but also for a quick clean of the floor, a quick swipe of a campsite table before you eat at it, a quick cleanse of the sink or the toilet seat... I know they aren't the most environmentally friendly item but they are a godsend in a camper van.
- **Wet wipes:** Much like the above. So useful for days

when you're not in a campsite and you don't fancy bullying the kids into the van shower.

- **Bananagrams, Dobble, Uno (and other small games):** There will be a lot of down time. These are games that the whole family can play and will kill some time as you while away the afternoon in another cafe or bar! (see section 4 for more info).
- **Lots of plastic boxes of exactly the right size:** If you have time before you set off, take care to really think about where you will store things in the van and which things you will need to access most often. Remember that as you drive, nothing at all stays put. Everything slides about and then tries to launch itself out of the cupboard at you the next time you park up. We found that once we had found plastic boxes of exactly the right size for the tiny gaps, life became much simpler and we got bumped on the head by falling trajectories much less often! We had a box on the shelf for the electronics devices and charging plugs etc, we had boxes in the food cupboards for snacks and old plastic takeaway tubs for the pasta/grains/rice etc which kept them from spilling all over the place. We had the things in the rear garage stored inside separate tubs so that we could locate everything more quickly.
- **Mattress protectors:** If someone is sick or a small child has an accident you will be eternally grateful for having covered their mattress with a protector. You can whip it off and then remake them a dry bed. Someone's mattress did get wet once and it took us an absolute age to get it dry in Springtime in Luxemburg....
- **A memory foam topper for your mattress:**

Motorhome mattresses are not made for sleeping on full-time. For an amazingly comfortable night's sleep we recommend a memory form topper from Duvalay. They will even make them to size for funny shaped beds. Ours made our fairly uncomfortable over-cab bed into a heavenly cloud of dreams! It also provided some well needed insulation on cold nights. Not cheap but worth every penny. http://www.duvalay.co.uk

- **Wet suits:** If, like us, you're heading out for a long time, there will be occasions when you're by the sea, or near a pool or a river and it's not quite warm enough to swim for any length of time. We had a family collection of cheap wetsuits and they allowed us to enjoy the outdoors so much more than we would have done without them. With a wetsuit you can swim in the Atlantic in November for longer than a few minutes and you can build dams in the river in the mountains for hours because you aren't developing hypothermia. Seriously- get some. You won't regret it!
- **A Kindle or other E-reader:** You will have lots of time for broadening your mind and reading. You will have no space in your van and no access to a library (or charity shops for your 50p bargain books!). Forget about how you 'love the feel of the pages under your fingers' and just get an Ereader! You can even download classic literature for free. Reading some Thomas Hardy or George Elliot can only ever improve your day!
- **Bicarbonate of Soda:** Flush some down your sinks every so often to dissipate stinky blockage smells. It's worth stocking up in the UK as I found it hard to locate in other countries. If you do get too stinky, you

can also buy tank freshener which you put a little of into your grey water tank-it breaks down the grease and deals with the odour.

- **Chocks:** I had never heard of these before but you will need a pair of triangular-shaped levelling blocks that you can place under whichever wheel requires a little boost in order to try and get your van as flat as possible. Sleeping on a slope can make you feel very funny (plus your dinner will roll all over the place!).
- **An insulating Windscreen cover:** A few months into our trip we realised that the silver cover we got with the van was not just for keeping the van cool in hot places but also for keeping us warm in the cold places. The windscreen is the least well insulated part of your motorhome and a lot of heat can escape through it. You can get internal and external ones. Ours was an external and it made a huge difference (it also often meant not waiting for the icy windscreen to thaw before setting off- another bonus!).
- **Bungee chords:** So useful in so many ways. Perfect for creating washing lines in the most unexpected of places and tying things shut when the handles break!
- **A power bank/portable charger:** This was s gift from my brilliant sisters- I had no idea such a thing existed. It means you can charge phones and other electronic devices even when you've got no electricity. PURE GENIUS- we would have really struggled without it.
- **A large mat/tarpaulin:** The places you are parked up will often be dusty/muddy/gravelly and a large mat outside your door (approx 5m/3m) allows

you a place to sit and play/eat/read without making everything filthy.

However you decide to use the information in this book, good luck on your travels, enjoy your children and be safe in the knowledge that following your dreams can lead you on the path to great happiness!

ABOUT THE AUTHOR

Jodi Hammond is a normal mum to three ordinary children. She grew up in suburban London in the Eighties. Because the internet hadn't been invented then, she spent all her time reading books and eventually became an English teacher. When their children arrived, Jodi and her husband went to live in leafy East Sussex where they muddled along until they decided to quit the rat race and take their family off on a big European adventure. For now, Jodi is back in the UK, spending most of her days dreaming up crazy plans for her family's next road trip.

25800088R00170

Printed in Poland
by Amazon Fulfillment
Poland Sp. z o.o., Wrocław